KV-577-959

HINDUISM

Patricia Bahree

B.T. Batsford Limited   London

Typeset by Tek-Art Ltd, Kent
and printed in Great Britain by
R.J. Acford, Chichester, Sussex
for the publishers
B.T. Batsford Ltd,
4 Fitzhardinge Street
London W1H 0AH

ISBN 0 7134 3654 9

Cover pictures
The colour photograph on the front cover shows
women decorating the floor with flowers for
Divali, Bombay, Maharashtra (the J. Allen Cash
Photolibrary). The photograph of schoolgirls in
Kerala, South India is by John and Penny Hubley.
The picture of Krishna is from the Victoria and
Albert Museum.

Acknowledgments

The Author and Publishers thank the following for
their kind permission to reproduce copyright
illustrations: the J. Allen Cash Photolibrary, page
38; Ashmolean Museum, Department of Eastern
Art, page 62; Barnaby's Picture Library, pages 22
(bottom), 28 (bottom), 42, 50; Bharatiya Vidya
Bhavan, page 49 (top); BBC Hulton Picture
Library, page 43; British Museum, page 21
(bottom); Camera Press Ltd, pages 13, 47; City of
Bristol Museum and Art Gallery, page 46; Mark
Edwards, pages 19, 61; Freer Gallery of Art,
Washington, page 31; Government of India
Tourist Office, page 5; Sally and Richard
Greenhill, page 67; High Commission of India,
pages 24, 45, 49 (bottom), 63; John and Penny
Hubley, pages 7, 8, 17, 21 (top), 22 (top), 26, 27,
32 (top), 48, 55, 58, 64, 65, 66; A.F. Kersting,
page 56; Keystone Press Agency Ltd, pages 16
(top), 28 (top); Patricia Mandel, page 30; National
Museum, New Delhi, page 6; John Ogle, pages 16
(bottom), 20, 25, 29, 37, 39, 53; Photographie
Giraudon, page 4; Press Information Bureau,
Government of India, page 14; Yogish Sahota,
page 36; Victoria and Albert Museum, pages 10,
15, 34, 40, 44, 52, 54. The pictures on pages 32
(bottom), 33 and 35 are copyright of the Author.
The pictures were researched by Patricia Mandel.

Quotations from the sacred texts are taken
mainly from Juan Mascaro's *The Upanishads* and
The Bhagavad Vita (published by Penguin) or
from the translations provided by A.L. Basham in
The Wonder That Was India (published by
Fontana/Collins).

Introduction

- This dictionary is an effort to guide those new to Hinduism through this fascinating faith. Hinduism is a very diverse religion. People worship different gods, for instance, and celebrate different holidays. However, there is a common core that most Hindus share. The basic beliefs of Hinduism, for example, include the belief in *Brahman*, the World Spirit or World Soul. *Brahman* is timeless and formless, the One and eternal. The many gods are all aspects of this One.
- The basic beliefs of Hinduism also include the caste system, which sets down how different groups in society should relate to one another. Long Sanskrit terms such as *varnashrama dharma* are also important to Hinduism. This term simply means the code of living based on a person's class and stage in life.

This dictionary covers basic concepts such as *Brahman* and caste, as well as Sanskrit terms such as *varnashrama dharma*. It also covers subjects of general interest such as festivals and marriages. It is hoped that this A-Z of Hinduism will help students and others quickly and easily to find out about specific topics, and that it will lead them on to discover more about one of the world's great religions.

Agni

The god of fire. In the Sanskrit language the word *"agni"* means fire. (It is related through Latin to English words such as "ignite" and "igneous".) The god Agni is present in every fire.

In the *Rig Veda*, Hinduism's oldest sacred book (in use by around 900 BC), Agni is one of the main deities, though he is not as important today. In this and later books he is seen as a link between people and the gods. The sacred fire is the centre of many rites. When offerings such as ghee (clarified butter) are placed in the sacred fire, Agni is said to consume them and carry them from this world to that of the gods.

Fire continues to play an important role in Hindu rituals. The Hindu marriage rite, for instance, takes place before a sacred fire; and at death the body is cremated and purified by fire. The cooking fire is important in the daily life of the home. Thus, Agni has remained important in the lives of Hindus.

In pictures and carvings, Agni is usually shown with three heads – with flames flickering behind them. His vehicle or *vahana* is the ram.

Agni, the god of fire, with his vehicle, the ram.

Ahimsa

Non-violence, non-injury to people and animals; doing no harm to any living thing.

The Buddha (c. 560-480 BC) was one of many Indian religious teachers who taught the doctrine of *ahimsa*. The idea that no living creature should be harmed is shared by various Indian religious groups – including Buddhists, Hindus and Jains. Monks of the Jain religion go to the extent of straining their drinking water and sweeping the path before them with a soft feather brush to avoid harming any small creatures.

Mahatma Gandhi made *ahimsa*, in the sense of non-violence, an important part of his struggle to gain Indian independence from British rule. (For further details, see *Gandhi, Mahatma*). Many Hindus are vegetarians because they believe animals should not be slaughtered for food. Though it affects some Hindus hardly at all, the ideal of *ahimsa* has influenced what many Hindus see as right and wrong behaviour. Non-injury to other living things is a widely accepted virtue.

4

Architecture

See *Temple*.

Art

Hinduism has inspired artists to create works of great beauty and power. The history of Indian art is very long, going back some 4000 years to the Indus valley civilization. Throughout this long period, Indian art has been mainly religious art. Gods and goddesses are among the artists' favourite subjects. Even when artists and craftsmen were making everyday items, they often decorated them with religious scenes. Combs, boxes to store jewellery in and playing cards were all adorned with figures of deities. There has, in fact, never been a clear division between religious and non-religious art. Statues on a temple, for instance, include not only gods and goddesses, but also scenes of people caught up in everyday activities and a wonderful variety of plants and animals, including an awe-inspiring array of mythical beasts.

Works of art that survive from the Indus valley civilization include a few small stone statues and hundreds of seals. The seals were stamped on goods to show to whom they belonged or who was sending them. These are often decorated with fine animal figures.

After the fall of the Indus valley cities, there is a long period from which few works of art survive. At this time, tribes of Aryan cattle herders were migrating into India. Perhaps their nomadic lifestyle meant they had few works of art. It is also possible that statues were made of wood and have rotted away.

The earliest large-scale stone sculpture was produced in around 300 BC. Fine early works were made during the reign of the Buddhist king Ashoka. The earliest known statues of Hindu gods and goddesses were made in the early centuries AD.

Stone sculpture reached a high point during the reign of the great Gupta dynasty (approximately 320-550 AD). The Gupta kings ruled a vast empire stretching across most of the Indian subcontinent. The Gupta period is often called the golden age of Hindu art and culture. In Gupta times the classical ideals of Hindu art were established. Later schools of art inherited the styles and standards arrived at in Gupta times.

During the Middle Ages hundreds of fantastic temples were built in India and stone sculpture flourished. Figures became more ornate and styles

A dancer carved in stone in painstaking detail. A graceful tree branch stretches above the dancer and musicians play at her feet. The statue was made to decorate a temple built some 800 years ago by the Hoysala kings who ruled an empire in southwestern India.

varied somewhat from one region to another. However, the basic features of Indian art changed little over the centuries. This is partly because religious works of art are governed by guidelines set down in ancient texts. The artist can use his creativity to a certain extent, but must work within the guidelines set down in these textbooks. Stone sculpture remains a living tradition, with beautiful statues still being made today within the ancient guidelines.

Painting is also a very old artistic tradition. Writings from Gupta times describe magnificent wall paintings, but none of these have survived. Some remarkably beautiful paintings, have been preserved on the walls of cave temples at Ajanta, some 300 kilometres from Bombay. (For further details, see *Temples*.) These paintings were done over a long period, with the oldest dating back to around the time of the birth of Christ and the latest to around 600 AD. Most of the paintings show scenes from the life of the Buddha. The Ajanta paintings are among the great art treasures of the world.

Miniature paintings were made to illustrate books. The oldest of these to survive dates back to around 1000 AD. When the Muslims arrived in India they brought paintings from Persia. Some Persian painters were also persuaded to come to India to work. European traders brought paintings and engravings from Europe. During the reign of the great Muslim emperors called the Mughals, a school of painting developed combining Indian, Persian and European ideas. Mughal painting reached a high point during the reign of the great emperor Akbar (1556-1605). Paintings were done in fine detail. Most were made to illustrate hand-copied books. Mughal paintings are full of life and colour and today are among the most prized paintings in the world.

Other schools of miniature painting developed at the courts of various Hindu rulers. Painters in Rajasthan produced bold paintings in bright colours. In the hills of Punjab, most local rulers employed a group of painters to produce pictures for them. One of the greatest inspirations was the stories of the god Krishna. The paintings are delicate, with graceful, flowing lines. They show Krishna as a naughty but lovable child and as a wonderfully handsome young man.

As well as stone sculptors and painters, Hinduism inspired artists in many other fields — among them, bronze casters, terracotta craftsmen and woodcarvers, to name just a few.

The villages of India, where over 75% of the population lives, are also centres of Hindu art. Folk art takes many forms. Scenes from religious stories are painted on the walls of homes, and statues of gods and demons are made for festival celebrations. Most folk art is made of materials that are cheap and easily available. They may not last a long time. Many statues and paintings are made new each year, to mark a holiday or a special season.

Krishna was a favourite subject of painters in the Punjab Hills in the eighteenth and nineteenth centuries. Here Krishna holds up the mountain Govardhan to shelter the villagers from a terrible thunderstorm.

Arti

An act of devotion in which an oil lamp is held before the image of a god or goddess and a circle of light is made in front of the image. Hymns may be sung as part of the *arti* ceremony. *Arti* may be performed at the beginning or end of other ceremonies, such as the regular *puja* in the home or temple.

Arti is performed during worship in a Hindu home in Leeds in the UK. The fire has been lit in a small metal dish held on a tray. A circle of light is made in front of the image.

Aryans

Nomadic cattle herders who began to migrate into India sometime around 1500 BC. Their homelands were probably in Central Asia, near the Caspian Sea. Some groups moved west across Europe, reaching as far as Ireland. (The word "Eire" is related to "Aryan".) Others moved into modern-day Iran (which also gets its name from the Aryans). Still others moved on into India. The migration was gradual, with various groups arriving at different times.

When the Aryans arrived in India, the great Indus valley cities (which were thriving around 2000 BC) were already in decline. In warfare, the Aryans had several advantages over the people living in India. They had weapons made of bronze which were superior to those of the local people. They also used horse-drawn chariots in battle, which were much quicker than carts drawn by bullocks or donkeys. The Aryans seem to have dominated the local people.

At first, the Aryans kept their nomadic lifestyle, pushing eastward into new lands. But agriculture, which required a more settled life, slowly took the place of nomadic herding. By 500 BC the Aryans had become a settled people and great cities had grown up along the valley of the Ganges river.

Over the centuries, Aryan religious and social ideas merged with those of the local people in India and with ideas brought by newcomers. All of these streams developed into Hinduism as we know it today.

In modern times, the word "Aryan" has been used mainly in connection with the German dictator Adolf Hitler. He felt the Aryans were a "master race", of which the Germans were part. However, Hitler's use of the word had more to do with politics and propaganda than with the people who settled in Europe, the Middle East and India some 2000 years ago.

Ascetic

A holy man. A person who builds up spiritual power by giving away all his worldly possessions and by learning to endure pain and control his mind and body. One who practises extreme self-denial as a means of religious discipline.

Ashram

A place where a religious teacher and his or her followers live together. A Hindu might go to an *ashram* to seek spiritual guidance or simply to get away from the bustle and cares of the everyday world. Some Hindus spend several weeks every year at the *ashram* of their *guru* or teacher. Others may never visit an *ashram* at all.

Ashramas

The four stages of life. Ideally, for a Hindu the path from childhood to old age should be made up of four stages or *ashramas*. These are that of student (*brahmacharin*), householder (*grihastha*), forest hermit (*vanaprastha*) and wandering holy man (*sannyasi*). Traditionally, the student lived in the home of his teacher and studied the ancient Sanskrit religious texts. The householder stage began with marriage. The householder raised children, supported his family and enjoyed life, while also carrying out the required religious duties and rites. Three goals are sometimes listed for the householder stage. These are *dharma* – following the sacred law; *artha* – getting wealth by honest means; and *kama* – enjoying the pleasures of life.

In old age a person left his home to live as a hermit in the forest. The *Laws of Manu*, an ancient religious text, says: "When the householder sees his skin wrinkled and his hair white and the sons of his sons, then he should retire to the forest . . ." (Manu 6.2). This is the time to turn his mind toward spiritual thoughts.

The final stage was that of the wandering holy man or *sannyasi*, who had given up his home and possessions, breaking his ties with this world in search of *moksha* or enlightenment. The word "sannyasi" means one who has abandoned everything.

Few men ever followed the four stages strictly. Women were never really expected to. Some women might accompany their husbands in the forest hermit stage, but a woman might also find a place in the home of her son, who would look after

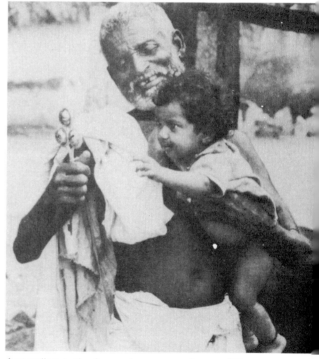

According to the four *ashramas* or stages of life, an old man should give up all his possessions and become a wandering holy man. However, a majority, like this man, prefer to find a useful place in the home of a son. Often older men and women living at home devote a large part of the day to prayer.

her in old age. Women were not encouraged to become wandering *sannyasis*, but some did and still do.

Today the four stages remain an ideal that is respected but not widely followed. Most men and women do not expect to progress beyond the householder stage. Those who do, however, are honoured.

The four stages offer a way of combining different goals into one lifetime. It is often said that the householder stage gives people a chance to enjoy life to the fullest, and then to ask, "Isn't there something more than this?" The answer is that the spiritual life of the third and fourth stages brings even greater happiness.

The four stages may also show the blending of values held by different groups in ancient India. The stages of student and householder seem to be Aryan ideals. The values of some non-Aryan groups may have stressed breaking ties with this world and seeking spiritual enlightenment. The four stages of life are a way of accepting and combining these different values.

Atman

The soul or self. The holy books, the *Upanishads*, teach that the World Spirit is present everywhere. It is in you and in all living things. It binds together all that lives. The World Spirit is called *Brahman*. The spirit within is called *Atman*. But they are both the same.

The *Atman* or soul is difficult if not impossible to describe. The *Katha Upanishad* makes the following attempt to put the indescribable into words:

The Atman is beyond sound and form, without touch and taste and perfume. It is eternal, unchangeable, and without beginning or end: indeed above reasoning. When consciousness of the Atman manifests itself, man becomes free from the jaws of death.

Avatar

(also spelled *avatara*). An incarnation of god on earth, especially of the god Vishnu. The word *"avatar"* means "descent"; literally, the descent of god to earth.

Most Hindus recognize ten *avatars* or incarnations of Vishnu. The most important of these are Rama and Krishna, the seventh and eighth *avatars*. Vishnu is widely worshipped in the form of these two gods. (See *Rama* and *Krishna*.) One of the clearest statements about the mission of the *avatar* on earth is contained in the sacred book, the *Bhagavad Gita*. Here, Krishna, revealing that he is an *avatar* of Vishnu, says:

> Whenever the Sacred Law fails, and evil raises
> its head,
> I take embodied birth.
> To guard the righteous, to root out sinners,
> and to establish the Sacred Law,
> I am born from age to age.
> (*Bhagavad Gita*, iv, 6-8)

All ten *avatars* were recognized in the sacred books of Hinduism by about the eleventh century AD. The list appears to have been built up gradually over the preceding centuries as new groups were added to the Hindu fold and local deities linked with the great god Vishnu. There are many stories associated with the ten *avatars*. All of them have a common theme: that good will triumph over evil with Vishnu's aid. In brief, the *avatars* and their stories include:

(1) *The Fish (Matsya)* Vishnu took the form of a fish, to save the sage Manu and the sacred books, the *Vedas*, from a great flood. The story is somewhat like that of Noah's ark, both being very ancient. The Fish tells Manu: "Those born of sweat, those born of eggs, or of water, and those living creatures which slough their skins – place them all on this boat and save them, for they have no protector." (*Matsya Purana*)

(2) *The Tortoise (Kurma)* In the flood the gods lost a very special drink called *amrita*, which preserved their youth and made them immortal. Vishnu became a great tortoise and dived to the bottom of the sea. A mountain was placed on his back and the ocean was churned by the gods, just as milk is churned to make butter. The *amrita* floated to the top of the ocean with other treasures, including the goddess Lakshmi.

(3) *The Boar (Varaha)* When a demon had cast the earth to the bottom of the ocean, Vishnu took

Vishnu (as Krishna) is shown in the centre, with his ten *avatars* around him. At the top: the fish, the tortoise and the boar. On the left: the man-lion and Rama, prince of Ayodhya. On the right: the dwarf and Krishna. At the bottom: Rama with the axe, Buddha and Kalkin.

10

the form of a boar, dived into the dark depths, recovered the earth and spread it out to float on top of the waters.

(4) *The Man-Lion (Narasimha)* A demon had gained the special boon that it could be killed neither by man nor animal, neither inside nor outside its home, nor by day nor night. It thus lived freely, causing great distress. To kill the demon, Vishnu took a form that was half man and half lion (thus neither man nor animal) and killed the demon on its threshold (neither inside nor outside its home) at sunset (a time when it is neither day nor night).

(5) *The Dwarf (Vamana)* Another demon gained control of the earth but Vishnu again thought of a way to bring its downfall. He appeared before the demon in the form of a dwarf and asked if he could have as much space as he could cover in three strides. The demon felt he could cover little land, and so agreed. Vishnu became a great giant and covered the entire earth and heavens.

This story is told with several slightly different endings. Sometimes it is said that in his three strides Vishnu covered the heavens, the earth and the underworld. In another version, he covered the heavens and earth, but left the underworld for the demons. In a third version, Vishnu covered the heavens and earth and then used the third stride to crush the demon.

(6) *Rama with the Axe (Parashurama)* At one time the Kshatriyas (the warrior class) became so powerful that they threatened to overthrow the Brahmins (the priestly class). Vishnu was born as the Brahmin Parashurama to right the situation.

(7) *Rama, the Prince of Ayodhya* Rama is one of Hinduism's most widely worshipped gods. His story is told in the great epic, the *Ramayana*, which recounts how he was banished from his land and sent to live in the forest, how his beautiful wife Sita was stolen by the demon king Ravana, and how Rama won her back and returned to rule as the perfect king.

(8) *Krishna* This *avatar* is perhaps Hinduism's most widely worshipped god. He was born in a palace but, out of fear of his wicked uncle the king, was taken to live in the countryside with a group of cowherds. He defeated many demons, even while still a child, and eventually killed his wicked uncle and ruled as a wise king. The stories about him are full of love – the love of devotees for their Lord, and the love that God returns.

(9) *Buddha* The religious teacher, the Buddha, is usually listed as the ninth avatar. Some texts say Vishnu was born as the Buddha to teach evil people wrong religious ideas. Others say he was born as the Buddha to save innocent animals, since the Buddha taught non-violence to all living things. Some lists of *avatars* avoid the problem by making Balkrishna, Krishna's brother, the ninth *avatar*.

(10) *Kalkin* The tenth incarnation is yet to come. At the end of our present age Vishnu will appear as a man riding a white horse. He will hold a flaming sword.

Some of the *avatars* are now rarely worshipped, though statues of all of them can be found in Hindu temples. Often the ten are shown together. Sometimes the list of *avatars* varies. Great sages and holy men of the past may be added to the list.

The idea of partial *avatars* also exists in Hinduism. Thus, any great or good person may be seen as a partial incarnation of god on earth. Many Hindus speak of their *guru* or teacher as an *avatar* in this sense.

Although *avatars* are associated mainly with the god Vishnu, occasionally the idea is applied to other gods and goddesses. For example, Sita, the wife of Rama, is often seen as the perfect woman. She is sometimes spoken of as an incarnation on earth of the goddess Lakshmi, Vishnu's wife. *Avatars* of Hinduism's other great god, Shiva, are also sometimes mentioned in religious books, but these have never had an important role. The idea of the *avatar* may have been associated especially with the god Vishnu because of his kind and loving character.

Banaras

A holy city and place of pilgrimage on the shores of the Ganges river. It is also known by the older name of Varanasi. Over a million pilgrims visit Banaras each year to bathe in the holy waters of the Ganges. Many temples have been built in this holy city. There are said to be over 1,500 temples in all.

Beliefs

Most Hindus will tell you that their faith is more a way of life than a set of beliefs. In fact, the great twentieth-century Hindu philosopher Sarvepalli Radhakrishnan has written that in Hinduism "what counts is conduct, not belief".

Hinduism's code of conduct is based on the idea of *dharma*, which is difficult to translate but is perhaps best understood as "duty" or "right action". Following one's *dharma* means being honest, kind and unselfish. It also means following the right course of action for you, which may not be the same as for others. The term *varnashrama dharma* is sometimes used to express this idea. It means doing what is right for you, based on the class you were born into and the stage of life you have reached. (For further details, see *Varnashrama dharma*.)

Hindu society is divided into four classes or *varna*: Brahmins (priests), Kshatriyas (rulers and warriors), Vaishyas (merchants and businessmen) and Shudras (workers who serve the other three groups). The large group of people who were not born into any of the four *varna* were traditionally considered outcasts or Untouchables. They did the worst jobs which were considered polluting to the higher groups, such as cleaning the streets. Untouchability is now officially illegal in India, but old ideas sometimes die slowly.

Within the four *varna* are many smaller groups often called castes or *jati*. Most castes are tied to one occupation, which is passed on from father to son. Thus there is a caste for barbers and one for potters. The four *varna* provide a sort of India-wide framework for the smaller castes. Each of these belongs to one of the four *varna*. (Also see *Caste*.)

The division of society into classes and castes is one of Hinduism's most important features. As far as caste is concerned, it is true that what one does is more important than what one believes.

Hinduism does, however, have some basic beliefs which most followers share. These include the belief in rebirth and the law of *karma*. According to the sacred books, the soul is born many times on earth. The body the soul will receive in the next life depends on one's deeds in this life. This is called the law of *karma*. *Karma* means "deeds" and it is one's deeds that determine whether the soul is reborn in a person of high caste or low caste, or in human or animal form.

The cycle of birth and death can be broken by gaining *moksha*, which means "release". This happens when the individual soul or *Atman* is merged with the World Spirit or *Brahman*. At this point the soul finds eternal Truth, Understanding and Bliss and is never born again.

Hinduism offers several paths to salvation or *moksha*. One of the oldest is the path of knowledge. By practising yoga and meditation, a person builds up greater and greater spiritual power. After years of effort spiritual insight may finally be attained. Salvation can also be reached by the path of devotion – by loving god with one's whole heart. A third path is the path of works. One can find salvation through working selflessly for the good of others, seeking no reward for oneself.

Hinduism is a religion that has grown up gradually over several thousand years. It has collected together the beliefs and rituals of many different groups of people. It is not surprising that Hinduism is a faith of great diversity. Just as people in different parts of India wear different kinds of clothes and eat different kinds of food, they also practise Hinduism in many different ways. In hymns and holy books, different religious practices are often described as rivers that all lead to the same sea. Thus, most Hindus have no problem accepting the various streams that flow within their faith. In fact, one of Hinduism's greatest strengths is that it is a flexible religion that allows people to follow different paths and still be a part of one great tradition.

To sum up, it might be said that Hinduism's code of conduct and basic beliefs can be divided into two large areas. Many ideas are based on *dharma* or social duty. These help people to build a well-ordered society on earth. The second group of ideas is focused on *moksha* or spiritual release. These lead the way to perfect Truth and Bliss, beyond the realm of this limited world.

Bhagavad Gita

One of Hinduism's most sacred books. The *Bhagavad Gita*, which means "Song of the Lord", is part of the great epic, the *Mahabharata*, which tells the story of the war between the Pandavas and Kauravas, two branches of the royal family. The

Bhagavad Gita, which was in use in its present form by around 100 BC, is often referred to simply as the *Gita*.

The setting of the *Gita* is the battlefield. The great warrior Arjun, one of the five Pandava brothers, sees his cousins and uncles, teachers and friends gathering on the other side. He believes in his cause, but rather than kill those he loves, he decides it is better not to fight at all. The god Krishna takes the form of Arjun's charioteer to tell him why he must fight. Krishna's lengthy and powerful speech brings together some of the most important teachings of Hinduism.

One of the main teachings of the *Gita* is the goal of "desireless action". Krishna tells Arjun that inaction – doing nothing – is wrong. People must act, but they should act without a desire for profits or rewards; they should work without attachment. Krishna says of himself:

There is nothing in the three worlds which I
   need,
Nothing I do not own,
Nothing which I must get –
And yet I labour forever.

He tells Arjun:

So, as the unwise work with attachment,
   the wise should work without attachment,
O son of Bharata,
   and seek to establish order in the world.

The importance of love, both of people for God and God for people, is also stressed in the *Gita*.

The *Gita* is sometimes called the "Hindu Bible", because of the important role it plays in the lives of Hindus. Many Hindus read from the *Gita* each day.

Bhajans

Devotional religious songs.

Musicians and singers walking from a temple to the Ganges river in the city of Hardwar. Singing *bhajans* or religious songs is an important form of worship in *bhakti* or devotional Hinduism.

13

Bhakti

Loving devotion to a personal god. It is *bhakti* that gives popular Hinduism much of its vigorous and special character.

In the *bhakti* stream of Hinduism images are important because devotion is offered to a personal god. Temples and family shrines are also important. Here *puja* is offered as an act of devotion. Hymn singing, telling the stories of the gods, religious drama, festival celebrations and pilgrimages are all part of the *bhakti* tradition.

Bhakti has produced a long line of great poet-saints who have sung the praises of Hinduism's gods and goddesses. Most of them wrote not in scholarly Sanskrit but in the languages of ordinary people. Their hymns are sung with great love throughout India.

Bhakti or devotion does not exclude offering older rituals that go back to Vedic times or seeking enlightenment through spiritual insight. But in *bhakti* it is love of a personal god that is most important. It is in the context of this great love that all other actions are performed.

Bhave, Vinoba

Often described as a living example of the Hindu ideal of selfless service, Vinoba Bhave (1895-1982) devoted his life to improving conditions in the villages of India. As a young man, Bhave left school to become a follower of Mahatma Gandhi and devote his life to serving the poor. In 1951 he started a programme to get land for landless labourers in Indian villages. He called it the *Bhoodan Yajna* or "Land Gift" movement and travelled across India on foot asking the rich to give part of their land to the poor. The word "*bhoo*" means "land" and "*dan*" means "a religious gift". The giver would gain religious merit and at the same time help to build a more equal society. Several million acres were given through the movement. Bhave was also active in setting up other programmes to help the poor, such as schools where disadvantaged young people are trained to help other villagers to help themselves.

Vinoba Bhave walking from village to village asking for donations of land for the poor.

Brahma

The god of creation. Brahma is often described as the first of the gods and the creator of the universe. Although he is seen as having created the universe, Brahma has few temples dedicated to him. Some religious books speak of the three main gods as Brahma (the creator), Vishnu (the preserver) and Shiva (the destroyer). However, today most Hindus belong to one of three great sects – worshippers of Vishnu, Shiva or the goddess or *devi*. Few in any Hindus have Brahma as their main god.

However, Brahma is still often seen on temple walls or in the religious pictures hanging in a Hindu home. He is often shown as the priest of the other gods. Brahma usually has four heads, as well as four arms. His vehicle is the goose or swan. He may carry various things. These include the holy book, the *Vedas*, a sceptre, a string of prayer beads, a water pot, a spoon used in making offerings in the fire sacrifice, or a bow. Brahma's wife is Saraswati, the goddess of wisdom and learning, sometimes also called Brahmi.

Several stories tell how Brahma came to have four heads. According to most versions, he once had five heads, but lost one. It is said that Brahma's wife, Saraswati, was so beautiful that he always wanted to look at her. She, however, was very modest and kept moving away from his gaze. Brahma decided to have four heads so that he could see her no matter where she was. She tried rising up in to the sky, but he grew a fifth head looking upward.

It is said that Brahma lost one of his heads in an argument with the god Shiva. According to one version of this story, it was burnt off by the fire of Shiva's third eye. This was because Brahma had made Shiva angry by speaking to him disrespectfully.

Brahma is sometimes said to have four heads to survey the four quarters of the universe, which he created.

A bronze statue of the god Brahma, made in South India in the eighteenth century.

Brahman

The World Spirit, eternal and present everywhere. The idea of the World Spirit had become an important part of ancient Indian religions by around 600 BC. *Brahman* is difficult for the human mind to grasp. In attempting to describe it, the great sacred books, the *Upanishads*, say:

> The Spirit supreme is immeasurable, inapprehensible, beyond conception, never-born, beyond reasoning, beyond thought. (*Maitri Upanishad*)

> There is a Spirit who is amongst the things of this world and yet he is above the things of this world . . . . He is beyond the life of the body and the mind, never-born, never-dying, everlasting, ever One in his own greatness. (*Maitri Upanishad*)

The world around us is always changing, but *Brahman* never changes. *Brahman* is sometimes described as a spiritual essence that lies beneath all things. *Brahman*, the One, eternal and unchanging, is present everywhere in the universe. *Brahman* is not only outside all things but also within all things that live. The *Upanishads* teach that *Brahman*, the World Spirit, and *Atman*, the individual soul, are in fact the same. Thus, there is a part of you and of everything that lives that is beyond decay and death. This part of you is beyond space and time and is not bound by the material world. The *Upanishads*, written in Sanskrit, say: "*Tat tvam asi*", meaning "You [the individual] are that [the World Spirit]".

In totally grasping this a person gains *moksha*, release from the cycle of birth and death. While it is possible to understand that the individual soul and the World Spirit are one and the same thing, it is difficult to truly experience this unity. Holy men and women may practise yoga and meditation for years to raise their spiritual level so that they can truly experience their Oneness with *Brahman*.

The *Upanishads* say:

> He who knows Brahman who is Truth, consciousness, and infinite joy, hidden in the inmost of our soul and in the highest heaven, enjoys all things he desires in communion with the all-knowing Brahman. (*Taittiriya Upanishad*)

15

Brahmin

(also sometimes spelled *Brahman*)   The highest of the four social classes or *varna*. Brahmins were traditionally priests, and many still are priests. However, today Brahmins do a wide variety of jobs.

A Brahmin priest conducting a prayer meeting. While Brahmins do a variety of jobs, many remain religious teachers and priests.

Calendar

The Hindu calendar, still in use for religious purposes, is based on lunar (phases of the moon) rather than solar calculations. Each lunar month has some thirty days and there are twelve months in all.

In ancient India the years were counted from 0 from the time an important king or dynasty began to rule. One group who ruled were called the Shakas. The national calendar of modern India is based on the Shaka era. The first year of the Shaka era is 78 AD of the Christian era. Thus, 1985 of the Christian era equals 1907 of the Indian national calendar. This modern Indian national calendar is based on solar calculations, though Hindu holidays are still set by the lunar calendar.

Caste

Hindu society is made up of many small groups generally called "castes". Castes have several important features. First, a person's membership in a caste is hereditary. Every Hindu is born into a caste group and has the same caste as his or her parents. Second, most castes have a set occupation. There are castes of barbers, potters, carpenters, etc. Third, Hindus almost always marry within the same caste. And fourth, all castes in a region are ranked one above the other. The castes at the top are considered the purest and those at the bottom are thought to be impure. (This is linked largely with the work a caste does. Jobs such as cleaning the streets or slaughtering animals are considered impure – thus, street cleaners and butchers are ranked very low.) Traditionally, a Hindu would not accept food from someone of a lower caste.

There are hundreds of caste groups in India. Each village, however, has only a few castes, perhaps ten in all. Most castes are spread only over

Caste is often tied to occupation. This potter belongs to the potters' caste . . .

16

... and this basketweaver belongs to the basketweavers' caste.

a small region. Thus the castes represented in a South Indian village would be different from those in a North Indian village.

As well as having hundreds of small castes (sometimes called *jati*), Hinduism also has four great social classes, called the four *varna*. At the top are the Brahmins (priests), followed by the Kshatriya (rulers and warriors), Vaishyas (merchants and businessmen) and Shudras (manual workers and servants). Outside the four *varnas* are a fifth group, traditionally known as Untouchables, who did (and often still do) the worst jobs.

The four *varna* provide an all-India framework for the small caste groups. Each of the smaller groups belongs to one of the four *varna*. Every Hindu, thus, belongs to a caste group and to one of the four *varna*. A man from the Punjab might tell you that his caste is Kutri and that he is a Kshatriya. A woman from Poona might say she is a Chitpavan Brahmin, giving her caste and *varna* standing.

The word "caste" itself is somewhat confusing. It is not, in fact, even an Indian word, but comes from the Portuguese "*casta*", which means "breed". Portuguese traders who came to India in the fifteenth century used this word for the groups in Indian society, and it eventually passed into English. The word "caste" is usually used to refer to the hundreds of small groups or *jati*. However, sometimes the word "caste" is (very confusingly) used to mean both the small groups and the four large *varna*.

The history of caste and *varna* is difficult to trace. It seems that the Aryans, who migrated into India around 1500 BC, had a three-level society made up of Brahmins, Kshatriya and Vaishya. The word *varna* means colour. It is possible that the light-skinned Aryans made up the top groups, while the darker-skinned local people whom they conquered became the Shudras and Untouchables.

Later, with the spread of Aryan ideas thoughout India, it is possible that new groups were brought into the "Hindu fold" as separate castes. Thus, a warrior tribe might become a Kshatriya caste. A trading community might become a Vaishya caste. In this way a local group could become a part of the growing religion, but still keep a separate identity.

From the outside the caste and *varna* systems look unchanging and permanent. It seems that there is no way for people to move up—or down—in the world. However, studies have shown that within the framework of caste things do change. For instance, sometimes it is possible for a whole caste to move up together. This is especially true if a low-ranking caste has managed to make money. Members of the group might then become land owners rather than workers. The whole group might change its habits and rites to copy those of higher castes. If the group is rich enough and powerful enough and good enough at copying the life-style of the upper castes, people in the area might eventually be forced to give it a higher rank.

In modern India a person can also change his status by leaving the village and getting a job or an education in town. There is no caste for bus conductors or computer programmers, so people from many castes fill these jobs.

The role of caste is often debated in modern India. The Indian Constitution outlaws Untouchability and discrimination on the basis of caste. Such laws are difficult to enforce, however. Many Hindus are against Untouchability, but in favour of the caste system. They point out that it has played an important role in village life in the past and that it continues to do so. Caste has provided a role and a job for everyone. Most castes have a caste council, usually made up of a group of elders. The caste council helps settle disputes within the caste. It also helps caste members who are in need, such as widows and orphans. In some ways, caste has helped villages to run smoothly and has kept life stable. Some Hindus say there is no point in throwing out the caste system, only to replace it with the class system of the West.

Other Hindus feel there is no place for caste in the Hinduism of the future. Caste, they say, keeps people unequal. They point out that many religious books stress the equality of all people before God. This is especially true in *bhakti* or devotional worship. Thus, they argue, Hinduism could continue to thrive without the caste system.

Cow, sacred

Cows have a special place in Hinduism. They are not worshipped, but they are well-loved and generally treated with care. They are not killed for meat. Many Hindus are vegetarians. Those who are non-vegetarian eat other kinds of meat, but few Hindus eat beef or veal.

Many Hindus are vegetarian because they feel it is wrong to slaughter animals for food. The special place of the cow is tied to *ahimsa* – respect for the sacredness of all life. The cow is sometimes thought of as a symbol of the earth, which gives, yet asks nothing in return.

There are also economic reasons for the cow's special status. In the Indian village the cow's milk, and the foods made from it – butter, ghee, cheese, yoghurt and many different sweet dishes – are essential for good health. It makes good economic sense to protect the cow and have a supply of healthy food year after year.

In small towns cows are often seen roaming the streets, eating the turnip or carrot greens thrown away by the vegetable seller or the grass along the side of the road. These cows are usually not stray animals. They have a home which they go to in the evening where they are milked. Tourists find the sight of cows on a city street amusing. But for the owner, who is probably too poor to own any grazing land, the cow is performing an important service by turning greens and grass that would otherwise be wasted into wholesome food.

Cremation

The usual Hindu funeral practice, in which the dead body is reduced to ashes by fire. The body is covered with wood, usually sandalwood if it is available. Funeral rites are performed by a priest and the pyre is lit by the eldest son, or by some other male relative if the person had no son. In cities, cremation is sometimes carried out in electric crematoria. Afterwards, the ashes are usually scattered in a river. Relatives often make a pilgrimage to the holy Ganges river to scatter the ashes there.

Cremation usually takes place on the same day a person dies. Soon after death, the body is washed and dressed in special clothes by family members. In a village or small town the body is laid on a stretcher and carried to the cremation ground. It is simply covered with a cloth, often bright red. In a city the body might be carried by family members and friends or a vehicle might be used to take it to the cremation ground.

If a river runs near a city or village, the cremation ground will be situated near the river.

Otherwise it is a special area some distance from the village or city that has been set aside for this purpose. Traditionally, the mourners taking the body to the cremation ground should be led by the eldest. Returning home, the youngest person leads the group.

Special ceremonies are performed for a number of days after the cremation. These are called *shraddha* ceremonies. For many Hindus the ceremonies last twelve days, but the number of days may vary.

Cremation is a very hygienic way of disposing of the dead, in that fire is an efficient purifier. It is also in keeping with the Hindu belief that it is not the body but the soul that is important. The body may perish but the soul is immortal.

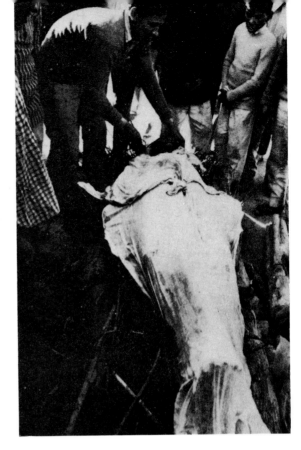

A body is prepared for cremation. The body will be covered with wood and the fire lit by the eldest son or some other male relative.

Devi

The goddess. While the word "*devi*" simply means "goddess", it is usually used to refer to the wife of Shiva, in all her various forms. In some of these she is mild and gentle and in others fierce and terrible. In her gentle form she is known as Parvati ("from the mountains"), Ambika ("the mother") or Gauri ("the fair one"). She is also the warrior goddess Durga ("the inaccessible"), who kills the evil buffalo demon. (See *Durga*.) In her most terrible form she is known as Kali ("the black") (see *Kali*) and Chandi ("the fierce").

For some Hindus, *devi* is the main deity. As *shakti*, or female energy, she is seen as the power behind the gods. Worshippers of the *devi* form one of the three main sects of Hinduism, the other two having Vishnu or Shiva as the main deity. (See *Gods and goddesses*.)

The goddess is widely worshipped in villages where she is seen as a protector of mothers and children. Most villages have a shrine for the *devi*.

Dharma

Duty, right action, the code of conduct that a Hindu should follow. There is a general *dharma* or code which applies to everyone and includes honesty, justice, charity, self-control, mercy and other such virtues. There is also a special code that can vary. This is the "*dharma* of class and stage of life" (*varnashrama dharma*). In this second sense, *dharma* varies with the class a person was born into and the stage of life he or she is at. Thus, the proper role in society for a Brahmin is not the same as that for a Shudra, and what is right for an old man is not necessarily right for a youth.

According to the *dharma* of class and stage of life, everyone has a job to do which contributes to the smooth running of society as a whole. No matter how lowly a person's station in life is, he or she must do the job assigned to his or her class and caste as well as possible. To try to do someone else's work only brings disorder and social chaos. The *Laws of Manu* say: "It is better to do one's own duty badly than another's well". The *Bhagavad Gita* adds: ". . . do thy duty, even if it be humble, rather than another's, even if it be great".

Dravidian

The languages spoken in South India are called "Dravidian languages". The four most widely spoken are Tamil, Kannada, Telugu and Malayalam. The term "Dravidian" is sometimes applied to people who speak any of the Dravidian languages. In this context, it usually simply means "South Indian".

The Dravidian languages are not related to the ancient language Sanskrit. Many scholars feel that the great Indus valley cities that were thriving around 2000 BC were built by people who spoke a Dravidian language. With the arrival of the Sanskrit-speaking Aryans in around 1500 BC, the Indus valley people were pushed southward. Thus, Dravidian languages are spoken today in South India and Sanskrit-derived languages in the North.

Modern Hinduism is often said to contain a mixture of Aryan and Dravidian beliefs and practices.

Dress

Hinduism does not require any particular type of dress; thus Hindus wear many different styles of clothing. There are many local and regional styles. The clothes a Hindu man wears depend largely on where he lives and what job he does. In cities in India most office workers wear trousers and a shirt. At home, an office worker may wear *kurta-pajama*. The *kurta* is a long, loose shirt and the *pajama* are loose-fitting trousers. The English word "pajama" comes from the Indian style of dress, but in India it can be used for street wear as well as bed clothes. Many men wear *kurta-pajama* to work. Young men

A turban can be an important part of a man's dress. Not all Hindu men wear turbans. Men of the Sikh faith usually do, but they tie their turbans in a different way. These elaborately turbaned Hindu men are wearing shirts and *dhotis* (partly hidden by the table).

A sari is the most popular style of dress for Hindu women. One woman has tucked her sari up between her legs to make the garment easier to work in. Most young girls wear skirts and blouses.

in cities often wear the traditional *kurta* with Western-style trousers or blue jeans.

In villages men often wear a *dhoti*, a single piece of cloth, usually white, wrapped round the waist and tucked up between the legs. Mahatma Gandhi wore this style of dress to identify with the villagers of India.

In the South, men often wear a *lungi*, a single, often brightly coloured, piece of cloth wrapped round the waist. The *lungi* reaches nearly to the ankle.

Hindu women usually wear a sari, a piece of cloth reaching from the waist to the floor and some six yards long. The sari is wrapped in different ways in different parts of India. It is worn with a short blouse called a *choli*. The end of the sari is left loose, flowing over the shoulder. A Hindu woman can use this to cover her head when entering a temple or when in the presence of family elders. In villages married women often cover their heads whenever they go out of the house, as a gesture of modesty.

In North India, especially in the Punjab, women wear the *salvar-kameez*. The *kameez* is a long, loose shirt that comes down to around the knees and the *salvar* are baggy trousers. A long scarf called a *dupatta* is worn at the neck and can be used to cover the head.

Women often wear lots of jewellery; for instance, bangles, rings, necklaces, earrings, ankle bracelets, toe rings and a nose ring. Jewellery is handed down in the family and is often given to a bride at the time of her wedding.

Durga

One of the names of the goddess who is the wife of the god Shiva. (For further details, see *Devi*.) Durga is one of her fiercer forms. Her role is that of the warrior goddess who destroys demons that threaten the world. A favourite story is her destruction of the buffalo demon, Mahisha. The demon was so powerful that none of the gods was able to destroy it. They, therefore, called on this beautiful goddess to do the job. To help her, each of the gods gave her one of his weapons. Durga is usually shown with ten arms, carrying Vishnu's discus, Shiva's trident and Indra's thunderbolt among other weapons. She rides on the back of a lion, who is sometimes shown helping her to slay the fierce buffalo demon. Durga is worshipped especially at the time of the Durga *puja*, which is usually celebrated in October or November.

Durga killing the buffalo demon. She carries the weapons given to her by the gods, including a bow, given to her by Vayu the wind god, and Shiva's trident (with which she stabs the demon). Her vehicle, the lion, is on the left.

Family shrine

Many Hindu homes have a family shrine where prayers are offered. A separate room may be set aside for the shrine or it may be set up in a niche in the wall or on a table in an out-of-the-way place. Several pictures or statues of gods and goddesses are used for the shrine. Incense holders and oil lamps are placed before the gods. Family members may worship at the shrine together or individually. The usual Hindu act of worship is the *puja*, generally a simple ceremony in which incense is lit, rice, fruit, sweets or flowers are placed before the gods, and prayers are offered. Foods placed before the gods are later shared by family members.

A woman in Tamil Nadu, South India, lights the tall brass oil lamp in front of the pictures in her family shrine.

Festivals

Hinduism has an almost endless number of festivals. However, some are celebrated only in certain parts of the country. Others are observed only by certain groups or communities.

Two holidays stand out as being especially important for most Hindus. These are Dussehra and Divali. The dates for holidays are determined by the Hindu calendar, in use since ancient times. It has twelve months, determined by the phases of the moon. The dates for holidays vary from year to year on the Gregorian calendar used in the West.

Dussehra falls in the month of Asvina on the Hindu calendar (usually October). Celebrations last for ten days. In North India, this is the time when winter crops are sown. On the first day, barley is planted in small dishes. By the tenth day, it has begun to sprout. The new plants are placed on the family shrine, and prayers offered for a good crop.

At the time of Dussehra people also celebrate the victory of good over evil. In Bengal, especially, the victory of the goddess Durga over the evil buffalo demon is celebrated in the Durga *puja*. Neighbours get together to set up temporary shrines to Durga. At the end of ten days, the statues of the goddess (often made of papier mâché) are carried in a long procession to the sea and submerged in its waters.

In other parts of India, Dussehra marks the victory of the god Rama (the seventh *avatar* of Vishnu) over the demon Ravana. This story is told in the great religious epic, the *Ramayana*. (See *Rama* and *Ramayana*.) A play version called the

Hindu communities outside India celebrate a variety of festivals, though sometimes celebrations take a slightly different form. This procession is taking place in the UK.

Ram Lila is acted out in villages and cities in ten nightly instalments. On the last night, Rama fires a flaming arrow into a giant bamboo-and-paper figure of the terrible Ravana. The figure has been stuffed with fire crackers and the audience cheers as evil is destroyed with a bang.

Divali is in the Hindu month of Karttika (usually November). It marks the return of Rama to become the rightful king. The word "Divali" comes from the Sanskrit word "*Deepavali*", which means "a row of lights". Rows of lamps or candles are placed in windows and along roofs and balconies to welcome Rama home. Fireworks are also set off on the evening of Divali.

Lakshmi, the goddess of wealth, is also worshipped on Divali. The woman of the house performs the Lakshmi *puja*, to bring good fortune. A lamp is left burning all night in most homes to welcome the goddess. Many Hindus play cards or gamble in some other game of chance on the evening of Divali, to attract good fortune.

Divali also marks the new business year. Businessmen open new account books and perform a *puja* to Lakshmi for prosperity in the year ahead.

Sweet shops are especially busy at the time of Divali. Friends and relatives visit each other and sweets are always offered. Boxes of sweets are sent as presents to the homes of friends.

Food

While Hinduism has few hard and fast rules about food, beliefs influence diet and food habits in a number of ways. Many Hindus (though probably not a majority) are vegetarian. This is mainly due to the belief that all life is sacred, and that it is therefore wrong to kill animals for food. Also, Hindus who grow up in a vegetarian household generally like vegetarian food better, and find it makes a healthy diet. Most vegetarians avoid eggs as well as meat, and some do not eat strong foods such as onions and garlic.

Many Hindus who are not vegetarians rarely eat meat in any case. Meat is expensive and difficult to keep, since most homes in Indian villages and many in cities do not have refrigerators. High-protein foods such as lentils are especially important in a vegetarian diet. Lots of milk and milk products are also eaten. A vegetarian dinner in North India might consist of a vegetable dish such as cauliflower and potatoes cooked with spices, a lentil dish called "*dal*", and homemade bread such as *chapati* or *paratha*. Dessert might be *ras malai* – made with cream, sugar, almonds and rosewater. In South India, rice would be served instead of bread and vegetables would be cooked somewhat differently. There are hundreds of regional styles of cooking in India.

While many Hindus eat meat at least occasionally, most do not eat beef. While all life is sacred, cows are held in special regard. The religious protection of cows is based on good economic reasoning. Milk and milk products are especially important for good health. These are available to most villagers as long as their cows are alive and healthy. (See *Cow, sacred*.)

Caste and the idea of ritual purity also affect eating habits. Traditionally, a Hindu should not accept food, especially cooked food, from a person of a lower caste. The higher you are in the caste system, the purer you are thought to be. Food touched by someone beneath you is considered polluted. For this reason, there are many Brahmin cooks in India. Since they are at the top of the caste system, the food they touch can be eaten by anyone. In modern India, especially in cities, ideas of food pollution have gradually changed. For instance, if a restaurant is clean and the food is good, most people would not ask about the caste of the cook or waiter.

Fasting is also a part of the Hindu faith, and many Hindus fast on certain holidays and at other times, as a religious discipline. Some devout Hindus fast one day a week – or more; others observe a partial fast, taking only liquids or special grains.

Gandhi, Mahatma (1869-1948)

The man who came to be called Mahatma or "Great Soul" was born as Mohandas Gandhi on 2 October 1869 in the town of Porbandar, in the present-day state of Gujarat. He became one of India's great twentieth-century political and religious leaders.

As a leader of the struggle for Indian independence from British rule, Gandhi stressed non-cooperation rather than terrorism or violence. He believed that "the peaceful and infallible doctrine of non-cooperation" was strong enough

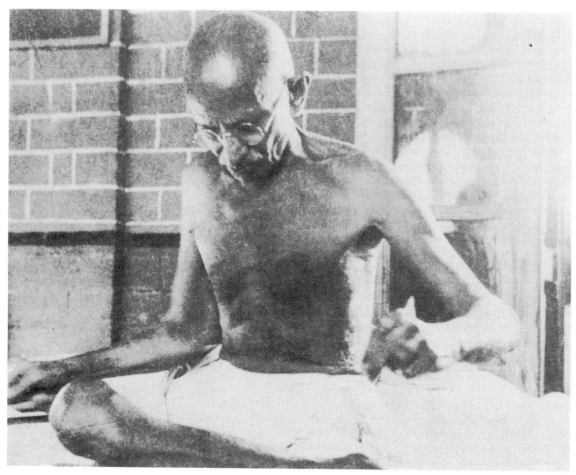

Mahatma Gandhi spinning cloth as part of his daily routine. Home-spun cloth or *khadi* became a symbol of the self-sufficiency Gandhi hoped India would attain.

"to paralyse the mightiest government on earth". In his non-cooperation campaign, Gandhi drew on ancient Indian ideals. Terms such as *"satyagraha"* ("truth force") and *"ahimsa"* ("non-violence") were part of the everyday vocabulary of the independence movement.

Believing that the demand for independence should come from the people rather than from a small group of leaders, Gandhi took up local causes. He fought to help poor peasants in Champaran district in Bihar and went to the aid of striking textile workers in the city of Ahmedabad. India had long been a producer of fine textiles, and Gandhi believed that the import of machine-made textiles from Britain was ruining the Indian economy. He urged people to burn all clothes made with imported cloth and to begin to spin their own cloth instead. Early in his political career, Gandhi discarded the English suits he had been proud of as a young man. He began to wear a simple hand-woven *dhoti*, the dress of the poor Indian peasant.

Gandhi had firm ideas on the kind of society India should have, once it gained its independence. He felt that the heart of India was its villages and that economic planning should strengthen the village rather than weaken it. He thought India would be wrong to ape the West by setting up large factories that would destroy traditional ways of living.

Religion was important to Gandhi and he became a great religious leader as well as an important politician. One change he wanted to see in Hinduism was the end of Untouchability. He called Untouchability "a blot on Hindu religion" and he and his followers travelled throughout India, working to remove it. Gandhi coined a new name for the people who had been considered Untouchable. He called them *Harijans* – "children of God".

While Gandhi was a Hindu, he wanted a secular India where all religions could be practised freely. He said: "I do not expect the India of my dream to develop one religion, . . . but I want it to be wholly tolerant, with its religions working side by side with one another."

In many ways, Gandhi was like a Hindu holy man. He dressed like a holy man in the simplest clothing, was a strict vegetarian living on a meagre diet, and owned few material possessions. In fact, in his autobiography, Gandhi wrote: "What I want to achieve – what I have been striving and pining to achieve these thirty years – is self-realization, to see God face to face, to attain *moksha*. I live and move and have my being in pursuit of this goal." But the path that Gandhi chose was not meditation and yoga but selfless service to society. He read daily from the holy book, the *Bhagavad Gita*, and urged others to read it and follow its ideal of desireless action. Gandhi once said: "Man's ultimate aim is the realization of God, and all his activities, political, social and religious, have to be guided by the ultimate aim of the vision of God. . . . If I could persuade myself that I should find Him in a Himalayan cave I would proceed there immediately. But I know that I cannot find Him apart from humanity."

Gandhi is remembered mainly as a political leader. But in his political work and his personal life, he drew on Hinduism's ancient teachings. As a religious leader, he took his faith in new directions.

Ganesh

The elephant-headed god, son of the god Shiva and the goddess Parvati. Ganesh, a jovial, good-natured god who can be approached without fear, is one of Hinduism's most popular gods. He is the overcomer of obstacles and will help his worshippers to clear any hurdles that may lie in their path. Thus, people pray to Ganesh before going on a journey, taking an exam, or beginning any important job. On visiting a temple, Hindus often pray first to Ganesh and then to other deities.

Ganesh is usually shown as short and pot-bellied, with four arms. He is fond of sweets and usually carries a bowl of them. He may also carry an elephant goad, a water lily or a conch shell. Ganesh's vehicle is a rat. It might be difficult for him to ride so small a creature, but in one way they make a good pair. While Ganesh can overcome obstacles with the strength of an elephant, the rat can move quickly and slip through tight places.

There are several stories of how Ganesh got his elephant head. According to one, Parvati made a small boy from the dirt on her body to guard the door while she was taking a bath. Her husband Shiva returned, was angry to find his way barred and cut off the boy's head. Parvati was very upset and to please her, Shiva agreed to replace the head with that of the first creature he found – which turned out to be an elephant.

Scholars of Hinduism have suggested that Ganesh may have originally been the elephant god of some tribe or group in India. When they were drawn into the Hindu fold, they brought their god with them, and he eventually found a place among the other gods, as the son of Shiva and Parvati.

Ganesh, the elephant-headed god, riding on his vehicle, the rat.

Ganges river

(also called the Ganga). Hinduism's most sacred river. All rivers are to some extent sacred in Hinduism. This is due in part to the importance of water in growing crops and in sustaining life itself. The Ganges river is considered especially holy. Many of Hinduism's most sacred pilgrimage spots are located along its shores. Among these are the holy city of Banaras and the town of Hardwar, located where the Ganges descends from the mountains to the plains.

Most Hindus would like to bathe in the Ganges at least once in their lifetime, since it is said to wash away a person's sins. Some sacred texts say that to die on the shores of the Ganges assures one of *moksha* or release from the cycle of birth and death. In old age some Hindus set out for the city of Banaras to die near the Ganges, be cremated there and have their ashes scattered in its sacred waters.

The Ganges is sometimes represented as a beautiful goddess, called Ganga. The goddess Ganga rides on the back of the *makara*, a mythical beast resembling the crocodiles that live in the river. In ancient stories the Ganges is said to spring from the toe of Vishnu, flow across the sky in the form of the Milky Way, and descend to earth through the hair of the god Shiva. He agreed to allow the river to flow through his hair to break her fall, which might otherwise have been too much for the earth to bear.

Pilgrims bathing in the Ganges river at Banaras.

Garuda

The bird on which the god Vishnu rides. Sometimes the Garuda is shown as part bird and part human.

Ghee

Clarified butter, i.e. butter that has been brought to boiling point, had the impurities skimmed off and then been left to cool. Ghee will keep for a long time, even in a hot climate. It is used for cooking and religious ceremonies, where small amounts of it are poured into the sacred fire as offerings to the gods. Such offerings are made, for instance, as part of the marriage ceremony.

Gods and goddesses

The idea of God exists on several levels in Hinduism. For most Hindus, the highest idea of the divine is *Brahman*, the World Spirit or World Soul. *Brahman* is without shape or form, present everywhere, changeless and eternal. *Brahman* is perfect Truth and thus beyond human understanding. No one could ever make a picture of *Brahman*.

For most Hindus, the many gods and goddesses are different ways of representing the divine. It is sometimes said that Hinduism has 330 million gods and it is sometimes said that Hinduism has one God. Both are right, because the many gods are all ways of seeing the One.

While the World Spirit is difficult to understand, the many gods can be pictured and prayed to. Worship in Hinduism is offered to these many gods. Among them, three are especially important. Most Hindus have either Shiva, Vishnu or the goddess (*devi*) as their main deity. The household shrine is dedicated to the family's main deity, and when the family visits a temple, it generally goes to one dedicated to its god. However, there is little strife between worshippers of these three great deities. In most neighbourhoods, worshippers of Shiva, Vishnu and the goddess live happily side by side. Most Hindus would agree that no matter which deity you worship, in the end, God is One. (For further information see *Brahman*, and also the names of individual gods such as *Shiva*, *Vishnu*, *Parvati*, *Lakshmi*, *Ganesh* and *Hanuman*. Also see *Devi* for information on the goddess.)

Gods and goddesses are a popular subject for calendars. This street-side calendar stall has not only the great deities but also popular heroes, important people and pictures of babies.

Guru

A teacher, especially a religious teacher and guide. Many Hindus have a guru to whom they go for spiritual guidance. The guru is usually a man, but may also be a woman. The guru may hold group meetings for his or her followers as well as talking with them individually. At such group meetings hymns are usually sung and the guru gives a talk on a religious topic. A person may consult his or her guru on everyday problems as well as spiritual ones. A guru may have only a few followers or several thousand.

In recent years many people in the West have become followers of Indian gurus. Two of the most popular are Maharishi Mahesh Yogi and Bhagwan Shree Rajneesh. Both the Maharishi and Rajneesh take at least part of their teachings from Hindu beliefs.

Swami Chinmayananda, shown here on a visit to London, is one of many Hindu *gurus* or teachers to visit the West.

Hanuman

The monkey god, widely worshipped throughout India. Hanuman, the general of a monkey army, brought his forces to the aid of the god Rama and helped him defeat the demon king Ravana. The story is told in the great epic, the *Ramayana*. Hanuman is loved for his selfless loyalty to Rama. In honour of Hanuman, monkeys are rarely harmed in India.

A holy man sitting near a Hanuman shrine reads from one of Hinduism's sacred books. Statues of Hanuman like this one are simply made and coloured bright orange. The statue has been clothed and garlanded with fresh flowers. The words "*Sita-Ram*" are repeated in Hindi behind the statue.

Harijan

The name Gandhi gave to the people who were considered Untouchables. It is usually translated as "Children of God". "*Hari*" means "god", especially Vishnu. "*Jan*" means "born of".

Harijan women and their children on a city street. The Harijans are India's ex-Untouchables whom Gandhi called "Children of God".

History of Hinduism

Hinduism is often described as the world's oldest living faith. It is a religion that grew up gradually over thousands of years. It has no single founder and no clear starting point.

Some of the roots of Hinduism seem to reach as far back as the Indus valley civilization, which was thriving in around 2000 BC. Its largest cities were Harappa and Mohenjo-daro on the Indus river in present-day Pakistan. Many statues of a female figure often described as a "mother goddess" were found by archaeologists in the Indus cities. She may be an ancestor of Hinduism's present-day goddesses. A figure sitting cross-legged like a person practising yoga appears on several seals. It

seems the Indus people stamped such seals on goods to show whom they belonged to. The cross-legged figure is in many ways like the great god Shiva, who is often pictured practising yoga.

Tribes from Central Asia who called themselves Aryans or "noble people" began to migrate into India by around 1500 BC. Other groups of Aryans settled in present-day Iran, and some migrated as far as Western Europe. Aryan religious ideas form an important part of Hinduism. The hymns of the *Rig Veda* were recited at Aryan religious ceremonies some 3000 years ago, in the early days of Aryan life in India. The *Rig Veda* remains one of Hinduism's most sacred texts. The four great classes or *varna* that still exist today were the basis of the Aryan social system.

In time, Aryan ideas were merged with those of the local people. By around 700 BC religion had begun to take a new direction in India. This is the time when the sacred books, the *Upanishads*, were composed. These are more mystical texts. Here the idea of the World Spirit or World Soul, called *Brahman*, is central. Rebirth and the quest for *moksha* or enlightenment are stressed. In about 500 BC the Buddha and Mahavira, two great religious teachers, were preaching in India. Their teachings were the basis of two new religions, Buddhism and Jainism. Hinduism, Buddhism and Jainism all spring from the same tradition and hold many common beliefs.

By around 400 AD the Gupta kings were ruling a vast empire that stretched over most of North India. Hinduism had by this time developed most of the features it has today. Great temples had been built. The sects of the great gods Shiva and Vishnu had developed. The caste system was the basis for social divisions. Untouchability also seems to have been practised. The great epics, the *Mahabharata* and *Ramayana*, were in use. Many scholars feel the term "Hinduism" should be used only from about this time onward. It is only from around the time of the Gupta empire that we can see most of the features of modern-day Hinduism working together.

The religious ideas that grew up in North India slowly spread to the South. The beliefs and practices of many local groups were added as the religion spread. Many local gods found their way into the great Hindu pantheon. Hinduism's great diversity is due in part to the way it developed. The *Upanishads*, the *Bhagavad Gita* and other works form the basis of a great religious tradition, of which there are many local variations.

South India produced a number of great saints

Ruins of the ancient city of Mohenjo-daro, in modern-day Pakistan. The Indus valley cities were built mainly of burnt brick. It has been estimated that some 40,000 people lived in Mohenjo-daro when it was at its height, some 4,000 years ago.

who wrote beautiful devotional hymns. It also produced some of Hinduism's greatest philosophers, such as Shankara (c. 788-c. 820 AD) and Ramanuja (c. 1017-1137 AD).

In the centuries that followed, much of India was ruled by non-Hindus who came from outside India. For several centuries most of India was ruled by Muslim emperors, and later India became a British colony. But Hinduism met the challenge of Islam and Christianity and remained the religion of the majority of the people. Hinduism has survived for such a long time, in part, because it is a flexible religion that can be practised on many levels. Leaders like Gandhi have shown that its ancient ideals can be used to meet new needs. Today, most Hindus do not feel that they need to choose between their ancient religious and cultural traditions and the demands of the twentieth century. Rather, they would like to think that Hinduism will be flexible enough to provide for whatever demands the future might bring.

The Buddha lived in India around 500 BC and founded a new religion. This statue shows the Buddha preaching his first sermon in the deer park at Sarnath near Banaras.

Horoscope

A diagram showing the position of the planets and the signs of the zodiac when a person was born. An astrologer uses a horoscope to forecast the future or examine the possibilities that lie ahead. A horoscope is drawn up for most Hindus shortly after birth. It may be consulted at various times. For instance, when a marriage is being arranged, the bride's and groom's horoscopes are given to a priest who compares them to see if they will make a good match.

A street-side vendor equipped to read horoscopes or to read palms. Both offer a means to try to see into the future.

Indra

In the *Vedas* Indra is a storm god, the bringer of rain who carries a thunderbolt (*vajra*) as his weapon. He is also a war god who destroys foes and demons and seems to have been an important god for Aryan warriors. In the *Vedas*, Indra is sometimes described as the greatest of the gods.

In later times, Indra's popularity declined. He is still often described as the "king of the gods", though few if any temples are dedicated to him.

Indra's vehicle is the great white elephant, Airavata, often pictured with four tusks.

Indra, riding on the great, four-tusked elephant, Airavata.

Kali

The fearful goddess who is the bringer of disease and war, and is the god Shiva's wife in her most terrifying form. Kali, whose name means "the black one", has black skin and wears a necklace of skulls. She usually has four arms and carries the severed head of a giant in one hand and an axe-like weapon in another. She is often shown with her tongue hanging out, dripping with blood.

It is said that Kali acquired her taste for blood when she killed a demon who had gained a special boon. Wherever a drop of the demon's blood fell, a thousand more demons sprang up. Kali killed the demon by stabbing him with a spear and drinking his blood before it touched the ground.

Animal sacrifices, now rare in Hinduism, are still performed at some Kali shrines. When the animal is killed, some of its blood falls on the image of the goddess.

For many Hindus Kali represents death and time. It is said that spiritual progress is only possible when one has come to grips with Kali and faced these unpleasant realities. In knowing Kali one knows the painful, frightening side of life and can overcome fear and pain.

The terrifying goddess Kali, carrying a severed head.

Karma

The effect of past deeds. The moral law that good deeds bear good fruit and bad deeds bad fruit. The law of *karma* is like a chain of cause and effect by which a person's actions determine his or her future in this life and the next. The word "*karma*" means "deeds", and it is one's deeds that determine future happiness or sorrow.

The idea of *karma* is tied closely to the belief in rebirth. Whether one is born rich or poor, in the form of a human being or lower animal, is the result of the deeds of one's past life.

Krishna

The eighth *avatar* of Vishnu and one of Hinduism's most widely worshipped gods. According to tradition, Krishna was born of royal blood but grew up in the countryside among the cowherds. His wicked uncle the king had been warned that Krishna would bring his downfall and he tried to have Krishna killed at birth. But the baby escaped by being secretly taken from the palace to the countryside to live with the cowherds. Even as a boy, Krishna killed many demons. But he was also a rather naughty child. He and his friends stole and ate the delicious butter that their mothers made.

Krishna grew up to be a handsome youth who won the hearts of all the village women. His favourite was the lovely Radha.

On reaching manhood, Krishna returned to slay his wicked uncle the king. He then ruled from the city of Dvarka. When the great war described in the epic, the *Mahabharata*, was being fought, Krishna helped the rightful Pandavas against the Kauravas. He agreed to act as the warrior Arjun's charioteer, in order to advise him. (See *Bhagavad Gita*.) Krishna's advice to Arjun forms the *Bhagavad Gita*, a part of the *Mahabharata* and one of Hinduism's most sacred texts.

Krishna has been a favourite subject of Indian artists over the centuries. There are many pictures of him killing demons, stealing butter and winning the heart of the beautiful Radha. He is shown with blue or black skin (his name means "the dark one") and he wears a peacock feather in his hair.

Krishna is generally seen as a god of love. Because of his love of mankind, he destroyed many demons. Out of love, he will help worshippers who pray to him. The Krishna stories show many ways that people can love God – as a mother loves a child, as a woman loves a man, or as a citizen loves a wise and just king. Krishna has been one of the main gods of the *bhakti* or devotional movement in Hinduism.

Krishna – in the centre, wearing a crown of peacock feathers – with his cowherd friends.

A SONG FOR KRISHNA

The love of the devotee for Krishna is the subject of many beautiful hymns. The following hymn is by Mira Bai, a Rajput woman who lived around 1500.

> I must absolutely see you,
> my sweet love.
>
> I think of you,
> I reflect upon you
> and I contemplate you.
>
> I go dancing
> on the dust of your feet
> wherever your steps
> descend on this earth.

From *Songs of Krsna* by Deben Bhattacharya, published by Samuel Weiser, New York.

Kshatriya

The second of the four great social classes or *varna*. Traditionally, Kshatriyas were rulers and warriors.

Lakshmi

The goddess of wealth and good fortune, and the wife of the god Vishnu. Lakshmi, considered the ideal of feminine beauty, is pictured as a lovely young woman. She is often shown sitting or standing on a lotus blossom.

Lakshmi is worshipped especially at the time of Divali in the Lakshmi *puja*. For many Hindus, Divali marks the end of one business year and the beginning of a new one. A special ceremony is performed in homes, shops and offices in honour of Lakshmi so that she will bring prosperity in the coming year. Most families leave a lamp burning all night on Divali to welcome Lakshmi to their home.

Some Hindu women wear a small gold image of Lakshmi on a chain around their necks so that the goddess will bring them and their families prosperity.

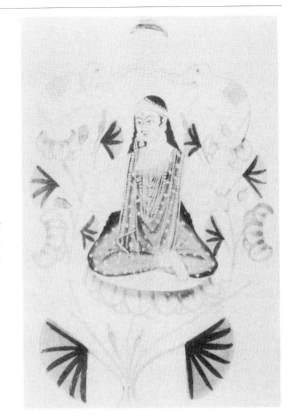

The goddess Lakshmi sitting on a lotus blossom. Two elephants lustrate her with water.

Laws of Manu

A collection of laws and guidelines for social conduct that was probably in use in its present form by the early centuries AD. Some material dates back to a much earlier age. The laws are said to have been written by a legendary sage named Manu.

The *Laws of Manu* and other ancient law books are called the *Dharma Shastras* and are part of Hinduism's sacred literature. They are classed as *smriti*, works which were remembered and handed down, rather than the more sacred *shruti*, that which was revealed by God.

The *Laws of Manu* deal with many subjects beside law and give an interesting picture of life in ancient India.

Mahabharata

One of Hinduism's two great epics. (The other is the *Ramayana*.) The *Mahabharata* has some 90,000 stanzas, which probably makes it the world's longest poem. It is the story of a great civil war in the kingdom of the Kurus, in the area around modern-day Delhi. On one side are the rightful Pandava brothers, supported by the god Krishna. On the other side are the Kauravas. The most sacred part of the *Mahabharata* is the section called the *Bhagavad Gita*, in which the god Krishna appears as the charioteer of Arjun, one of the Pandava brothers. Although he is a great warrior, Arjun does not want to kill the friends and relatives gathering on the other side of the battlefield. He says he would rather lay down his arms and be killed. Krishna urges the despairing Arjun to fight, and in doing so brings together, in his long and beautiful speech, many of the basic beliefs of Hinduism.

The *Mahabharata* was probably in use in its present form by the early centuries AD. Parts of it, however, are much older. It is likely that the story is based on a real war, which may have taken place as early as the ninth century BC.

Mantra

A word formula repeated over and over to aid meditation, raise the level of consciousness and evoke the inner presence of God.

Marriage

The Hindu marriage ceremony is performed by a Brahmin priest and takes place before a sacred fire, which is usually lit in a special metal vessel. The ceremony is in Sanskrit, the language of ancient India, and usually lasts several hours. In the most important part of the ceremony, the bride's sari and groom's *kurta* (shirt) are tied together and the two walk around the sacred fire seven times.

Marriages are not held in a temple. The ceremony usually takes place at the bride's home, often out-of-doors in the courtyard or garden. Sometimes the village square or local park is used for weddings.

Most marriages are arranged by the parents, and the bride and groom may meet for the first time at the ceremony. Generally, Hindu teenagers are happy to leave the choice to their parents. They know their parents love them and feel that, with their greater experience, they will choose a good marriage partner. The bride and groom will be from the same caste group and the same economic background, so the adjustment to married life should be easier. In arranged marriages the idea is that love should come after marriage, not before. The large number of happy Hindu marriages would tend to show that the system often works quite well.

Before the wedding, the bride's and groom's horoscopes will be shown to a priest who will compare them to see if the two will make a good match. The day and time of the wedding will also be set by the priest, who will determine the most auspicious moment by studying the horoscopes. A wedding may be held at 10 am or 10 pm, or even 2 am.

The colour for brides in India is red. The bride usually wears a red sari trimmed with gold. She also wears lots of gold jewellery. She may wear special make-up, with beautiful patterns across her forehead and around her eyes. This is applied before the ceremony and washed off afterwards. She may also have decoration on the palms of her hands and soles of her feet. This is made with a special plant called *mehndi* and lasts for around a month.

The groom may wear *kurta-pajama* (a long, loose

This Hindu wedding is taking place in Britain. The priest is on the right. The bride and groom are making offerings of small amounts of grain by placing them in the sacred fire.

36

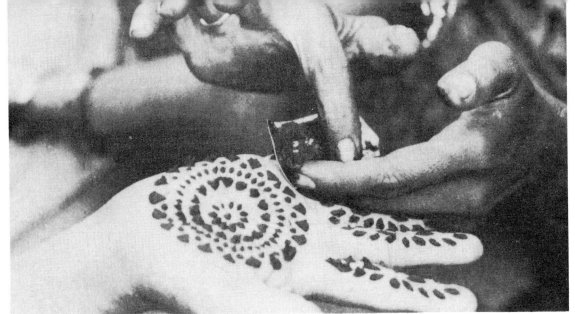

shirt with loose-fitting trousers) or other Indian dress, or a Western suit. He usually wears a special turban with a veil made of chains of flowers covering his face. Traditionally, the groom should arrive at the bride's house, riding on horseback, at the head of a procession of friends and relatives. Today, however, he often arrives in a car decorated with chains of marigolds and other flowers.

After the ceremony, the bride and groom will usually go to live with the groom's family.

The bride's hands are often specially decorated for the wedding. A plant called *mehndi* is ground up into a paste, and patterns are made on the palm of the hand. When the paste is washed off, it leaves a red dye behind. The red pattern lasts about a month.

Mira Bai

A Rajput woman who lived around 1500 and wrote devotional hymns to the god Krishna. The main theme is her great love of God. Not much is known about the life of Mira Bai. It is said that she was the daughter of one of the local rulers in Rajasthan. When her husband died, she devoted all her efforts to serving Krishna. Today, Mira Bai's hymns are among the favourite hymns of many Hindus.

Moksha

Release from the cycle of birth and death. "*Moksha*" means "release", "liberation", "freedom". The *Upanishads* and other sacred texts teach that the soul is born many times on earth. It is caught in an endless cycle of birth and death. The most important spiritual aim is to break free, to attain *moksha*, and cut all earthly ties forever, never to be born again. This happens when the individual soul (*Atman*) is merged with the World Soul (*Brahman*). Having attained *moksha*, the soul exists forever in a state of perfect bliss and perfect truth. Describing the quest for *moksha*, the *Mundaka Upanishad* says:

As rivers flowing into the ocean find their final peace and their name and form disappear, even so the wise become free from name and form and enter into the radiance of the Supreme Spirit who is greater than all greatness.

Music and dance

In the Middle Ages most of the great Hindu temples had groups of musicians and dancers who performed for the gods. The temple and the palace were the places where most musicians and dancers found employment and where music and dance developed and flourished.

Indian classical music grows out of an ancient musical system. At the heart of the system is the *raga*, a series of five or more notes on which the melody is based. There are six separate *ragas*. The musician can improvise within the framework of the *raga*.

Each of the *ragas* is suited to a certain time of day. Each also has a special emotional feel. Thus, *Megha Raga*, which is associated with peace and calm, is to be played in the morning, and *Hindola Raga*, which is associated with love, is to be played at night. Various meters or *talas* may be used. The programme for a modern concert lists the *raga* and the *tala* for each piece played.

Today, there are three main styles of classical Indian dance. Among the oldest is *Bharata Natya*. The various postures and gestures of this dance style are described in a book on dance, the *Bharata Natyashastra*, which was in use by the early centuries AD. Movements in *Bharata Natya* are angular and symmetrical. The dancer moves with great speed to create a fascinating array of body patterns. The neck and eyes are as important as the arms and legs. The *Bharata Natyashastra*, for instance, mentions nine different postures for the neck and thirty-six eye movements. Hand gestures, called *mudras*, are especially important. Each carries a meaning, and the dancer can string them together to tell a story or evoke a mood.

A second and very different type of dance is *Kathakali*, a form of dance drama. *Kathakali* comes from Southwest India, along the Malabar coast. Stories from the great epics, the *Ramayana* and *Mahabharata*, are often acted out. The dancers wear elaborate costumes and make-up and fantastic masks. Various gestures of the eyes, hands and other parts of the body are as important in *Kathakali* as they are in *Bharata Natya*.

A third type of dance is *Kathak*. This style was developed in North India. It is less angular and more flowing than *Bharata Natya*. *Kathak* began as a temple dance, but was developed further at the courts of Muslim rulers.

As well as classical music and dance, there are numerous styles of folk music and dance performed in villages throughout India.

While most concerts of classical music and dance

This Bharata Natya dancer is depicting the god Shiva as Lord of the Dance. Her right hand makes the gesture for the deer, which Shiva is often shown holding. The deer represents love and passion. The left hand makes the gesture for fire, which has the power to destroy.

38

are today performed in modern auditoria and not temples, music is still a part of temple worship. Hymn singing is especially important in devotional Hinduism. Worshippers may gather in temples in cities and villages on one or several evenings a week to sing hymns in praise of Krishna, Rama and Shiva.

Several Hindu gods have a special association with dance and music. The beautiful goddess Saraswati is the patron of art, music and learning. She carries a *veena* (a stringed musical instrument) and a book.

Shiva is sometimes known as Nataraja – Lord of the Dance. He is shown dancing in a circle of flame. The dance here has a symbolic meaning. It is said that it is the energy of Shiva's dancing that creates the world and then preserves it through many eons. It is the energy of the dance, for instance, that makes day follow night and summer follow winter. After millions of years Shiva's dancing will become wild and fierce, and as it grows faster and fiercer, the energy of this wild dancing will destroy the world. Then the world will be created again, through the energy of Shiva's dance.

Om

A holy syllable. For many Hindus, *Om* stands for the whole universe and its Oneness. It represents *Brahman*, the World Spirit. It is sometimes understood simply as meaning "Yes", in the sense of "Yes, there is an eternal Being behind the ever-changing world".

Om is also a symbol of spiritual good. Hindus like to have it somewhere in their homes, perhaps on a poster or a plaque that is part of the family shrine. It is also found on practical things like a paperweight or night-light. Many Hindus wear it on a pendant round their necks.

Om is often used as part of a *mantra*, and it may be written at the beginning of sacred books.

The symbol *Om* written above an enclosure which holds the image of a god. The name of the god is written at the top in Hindi.

Parvati

The goddess in her kind and gentle form. (See *Devi*.) The wife of Shiva and mother of the gods Ganesh and Karttikeya. Parvati means "from the mountains". She gets her name from her father, Himavan, god of the Himalayas. Parvati is pictured as a beautiful woman. Her vehicle is the lion.

One interesting story about Parvati tells how she won the attention of the god Shiva, whom she wanted to marry. At first she thought that seeing her great beauty, he would soon try to win her heart. But as time passed and Shiva failed to notice her, she realized that she would have to take some action. She decided to send Kama, the god of love, to shoot his arrows of passion at Shiva's heart. When Kama arrived, Shiva was deep in meditation. He was so angry at being disturbed that he opened his third eye and burnt Kama to a cinder. However, an arrow had already struck his heart, and he became more interested in Parvati. Still, however, he preferred to meditate.

Parvati decided to take up meditation herself. Then she started to follow the practices of an ascetic or holy person. She ate almost no food and tortured her body to learn to overcome pain. As her spiritual power grew, she succeeded in winning Shiva's attention.

One day a Brahmin priest came to her and asked her why she was torturing her beautiful body. She said she was trying to get the attention of Lord Shiva, whom she wanted to marry. The Brahmin asked why she should want to marry Shiva. He was not one of the handsome gods. He spent his time meditating in cremation grounds. He wore frightening snakes around his body. Like a holy man, he had no home and begged for food. He was dirty and covered his body with ashes. Parvati refused to listen. She said she loved Shiva and would have no one else.

Then the Brahmin revealed that he was Shiva himself in disguise and that he had been testing Parvati. Soon after, Shiva and Parvati were married.

The goddess Parvati holds her son Karttikeya on her lap. Her other son, the elephant-headed god Ganesh, helps his father, the god Shiva, string severed heads. The family sits on the edge of a cremation ground.

The severed heads, the cremation fires and the skeleton in the foreground are reminders that the span of human life is short, and death and rebirth are certain for those who have not attained liberation.

Paths to salvation

Hinduism offers a number of ways in which a person may attempt to reach God. It is often said that because people are different, the kind of religious life that suits one may not suit another. A person should find the path that is best for her or him. No one way is necessarily better than the other.

One important path is that of meditation and knowledge (*jnana*). A person gains spiritual insight after years of effort and discipline, during which spiritual power is gradually built up. The path of knowledge is followed, for instance, by the holy man who retires to the forests of the Himalayas to practise yoga, meditate and seek spiritual truth.

The path of devotion (*bhakti*) is taken by a larger number of Hindus. Salvation is reached by loving God with one's whole heart.

The path of work (*karma*) is another possibility. This could mean simply doing the right work according to one's caste and performing all the required rituals. The *Bhagavad Gita*, however, stresses the importance of desireless action, of working without seeking rewards. For Gandhi and many other modern Hindus, this has meant seeking salvation through serving one's fellow human beings.

While these are seen as three separate paths, they might all influence a person's life. A Hindu today might work selflessly to improve society and also offer loving devotion to God. He or she might also recognize the existence of the World Spirit and the possibility of gaining *moksha* or release through the path of knowledge and spiritual insight.

Philosophy (Six Systems of)

Debate on philosophical subjects was a favourite intellectual pastime in ancient India. By the early centuries AD, six separate systems of philosophy had developed. Of these, the Vedanta school has had the greatest influence over the centuries. Vedanta is based on the teachings of the *Upanishads*. Its central theme is *Brahman*, the World Soul. One of the most famous philosophers of the Vedanta school was Shankara, who lived and taught in South India in the eighth and ninth centuries. Most Indian philosophers today belong to one of the sub-schools of Vedanta.

All of the schools of philosophy are based on complicated ideas. Only a brief indication of what they stress can be given here. The six schools are:
(1) *Nyaya*, which emphasizes logic.
(2) *Vaisheshika*, which emphasizes cosmology and argues that all material things are made up of four kinds of atoms, earth, water, fire and air.

(3) *Samkhya*, which teaches that there are two basic categories in the universe – matter (*prakriti*) and soul (*purusha*). *Samkhya* offers a theory of the creation of the universe from these two. *Samkhya* teachers also developed the theory of the three qualities (*gunas*): virtue (*sattva*), passion (*rajas*) and dullness (*tamas*). *Sattva* is present in people who are truthful and wise; *rajas* in those who are violent or energetic; and *tamas* in those who are dull, stupid or gloomy.
(4) *Yoga*, which emphasizes spiritual discipline and is related to the yoga exercises practised today.
(5) *Mimamsa*, which emphasizes the importance of the *Vedas* and Vedic ritual.
(6) *Vedanta*, which emphasizes the teachings of the *Upanishads* and the existence of the World Soul. The ultimate purpose of existence is the union of the individual soul with the World Soul through the attainment of *moksha*.

Pilgrimage

Hindus go on pilgrimages for many reasons. Most feel that they gain religious merit by visiting one of the religion's sacred places. Some people go to fulfil a vow, others because they hope the visit will bring wealth and prosperity to their family. Many go simply out of devotion.

There are hundreds of places a pilgrim might visit. These include sacred rivers such as the Ganges and spots high in the awe-inspiring Himalayas. Great temples are also places of pilgrimage.

Pilgrimage places can be grouped into two main types. Many are natural creations such as rivers and mountains. These may be considered sacred because of their great importance to life or because they are particularly beautiful or inspire awe and wonder. A second type of pilgrimage spot includes man-made structures or places associated with important events. Great temples and places where famous teachers taught make up this group. Sometimes the two overlap. For instance, many great temples have been built along the Ganges

river. Pilgrims visit both the river and the nearby temples.

Huge crowds gather at pilgrimage spots for special festivals. The Kumbh Mela, held every twelve years at the place where the Ganges and Jamuna rivers meet, draws one of the largest crowds – over 2 million pilgrims. Several hundred thousand people attend the festival held each year at the Jaganatha temple in the city of Puri. (The English word "juggernaut", meaning a large vehicle, comes from the gigantic temple car on which Lord Jaganatha, a form of Vishnu, rides in procession.)

Pilgrims pull the temple car carrying Lord Jaganatha through the streets of the city of Puri. Lord Jaganatha is a form of the god Vishnu. Several hundred thousand pilgrims gather for the annual festival honouring him.

Pradakshina

Walking around (or circumambulating) a shrine as an act of devotion. The shrine is kept on the right.

Puja

Worship. An act of worship performed at home at the family shrine or in a temple. At home, *puja* is often a simple ceremony. An oil lamp and incense sticks are lit at the shrine. Offerings of coconut, fruit, sweets, rice or other foods are made to the deity. Water may be sprinkled on the image of the deity. Prayers are offered. The food presented to the deity is later shared by family members.

Puja offered in a temple is similar, though the ceremony may be more elaborate. (For details, see *Temple*.)

Whether at home or in a temple, *puja* has three main parts. The first is giving the offerings to the deity. The second is viewing the image of the deity. This is called taking *darshan* of the deity. At some temples the deity can be viewed only at certain times. The third part is taking *prashad*. Here part of the offerings given to the deity are taken and eaten by the worshipper. *Prashad* may also be given to the poor or to friends and family.

Puranas

Sacred books of Hinduism that contain many of the best-known stories of the gods and goddesses. The stories were passed on orally for centuries before they were written down. The word "*Purana*" literally means something very old. These stories were already ancient when they were compiled into books by Brahmin priests. There are eighteen major *Puranas*. Some of these existed in their present form by around 400 AD. Others may date from 1000 AD or later.

Radhakrishnan, Sarvepalli (1888-1975)

India's second president and one of the greatest Hindu philosophers of the twentieth century. Radhakrishnan taught at several Indian universities as well as Oxford University in England. He was appointed to the largely ceremonial position of President of India in 1962. Radhakrishnan became, in a sense, an "ambassador of Hinduism" in the West, attempting to explain the Hindu religion to people outside India. His books include great works of scholarship on Indian philosophy as well as easy-to-read introductions to Hinduism for Western readers. Among the latter, one of the most popular is his short book *The Hindu Way of Life*.

Sarvepalli Radhakrishnan, on the right, chats with another religious leader. Radhakrishnan, one of Hinduism's greatest modern philosophers, also held the mainly ceremonial position of President of India.

Rama

The seventh *avatar* of Vishnu, and one of Hinduism's most widely worshipped gods. The story of Rama is told in the great epic, the *Ramayana*.

Rama was the eldest and most capable son of King Dasharatha of Ayodhya and should have been next on the throne. However, one of the king's wives reminded him that years earlier he had offered her one wish. She asked that her son Bharata be made the next king and that Rama be banished to the forest for fourteen years.

The king kept his word. Bharata was named heir and Rama, his wife Sita, and his brother Lakshman left the palace to live in the forest. At Rama's departure, the people of Ayodhya and Bharata himself were full of sorrow. When the old

> FROM THE RAMAYANA
>
> Describing the final battle between Rama and Ravana, the *Ramayana* says:
>
> Then Rama . . . took his flaming arrow like a hissing snake . . . .
> Enraged he fiercely bent his bow against Ravana, and intent on his mark, he shot the entrail-tearing arrow . . . .
> Bearing the death of the body, the arrow flew with great speed, and tore through the heart of the evil-working Ravana.

king died, Bharata put Rama's sandals at the foot of the empty throne and said he would rule only as Rama's representative until he returned.

Meanwhile, in the forest, the terrible demon Ravana kidnapped the beautiful Sita, carrying her off to his palace in Lanka (identified with modern Sri Lanka or Ceylon, the island off the tip of South India). Rama and Lakshman set off to rescue her. They were aided by the monkey general Hanuman and his army of monkeys. At last, Rama killed Ravana and freed Sita. By now, the fourteen years' banishment was over. Rama, Sita and Lakshman returned to Ayodhya, where Rama became the rightful king.

Much has been written about the *Ramayana*. Rama was probably a real king who lived in about the seventh or eighth century BC. Many of the places he visits on his trip south to rescue Sita have been identified as real places. Some scholars feel that the monkey army was perhaps an army of tribal people who lived in the forest and came to Rama's aid.

It has also been suggested that the story of Rama is actually the story of the spread of Aryan religion and culture to South India. Rama, thus, represents the ideal Aryan king who gains power over Ravana, who stands for the South with all its dangerously different customs and ideas.

The story of Rama is important today, in part, because of the values it teaches. Rama is both the ideal man and the ideal king. He is honest, trustworthy and loyal. He obeys his father's wishes and is able to see that this will bring the long-term good. Sita is the ideal wife – totally devoted to her husband. Lakshman is the ideal brother – giving up palace life and braving the dangers of the forest out of loyalty to Rama. When Rama returns to Ayodhya he is not only the rightful king, but establishes an ideal government. During his rule, justice, truth, prosperity and happiness prevail. In India, the concept of ideal government is often called *Rama-raja*, the rule of Rama. (See *Ramayana*.)

The god Rama on horseback. Rama is an incarnation of the god Vishnu and one of Hinduism's most widely worshipped gods.

Ramakrishna (c. 1834-1886)

A Hindu saint and mystic. As a young man, Ramakrishna was a temple priest in a Kali temple near Calcutta. He was an ardent devotee of the *devi* or goddess. Ramakrishna experienced extremely powerful mystical visions. He appears to have been able to reach extraordinary states of consciousness.

Ramakrishna studied various religions, including Christianity and Islam. In each case, he tried to totally experience the religion. In the end, he decided that all religions were true and called them all variant paths to the same goal, which is union with God.

As Ramakrishna's popularity grew, thousands of people travelled to Calcutta to hear him speak. The Ramakrishna Mission, which bears his name, was founded by his disciple, Vivekananda. It now has branches throughout the world.

Ramakrishna, the nineteenth-century saint, worshipped the goddess Kali but also attempted to discover the nature of other Hindu deities and the meaning of Western religions.

Ramanuja (c. 1017-1137)

A Hindu philosopher and teacher. One of the most important thinkers and writers on *bhakti* or devotional Hinduism, Ramanuja is often said to have provided the intellectual basis for the *bhakti* movement. Ramanuja rejected the importance of an impersonal god. Instead, religion for him meant loving devotion to the god Vishnu, whom he describes in personal terms as compassionate, tender, loving, generous, etc. His writings conflict to some extent with those of the great philosopher Shankara. Shankara's teachings are sometimes called "monist" because they stress the Oneness of the World Spirit. Ramanuja is described as a "qualified monist".

Ramanuja taught in the great temple at Shrirangam in South India. From here he travelled to many parts of India, debating and discussing his ideas.

Ramayana

The great epic which tells the story of Rama, Prince of Ayodhya, the seventh *avatar* of Vishnu. (See *Rama*.) There are two important versions of the *Ramayana*. The older was written in the Sanskrit language by a scholar called Valmiki, who probably lived sometime between 200 BC and 200 AD. It is thought Valmiki based his great work on hero stories that were well-known and had been handed down orally for centuries.

The second and more popular version of the *Ramayana* was written in the seventeenth century in Hindi, the major language of North India today, by the poet Tulsi Das. In the Tulsi Das *Ramayana* it is clear that Rama is not simply a great hero of the past but an *avatar* of Vishnu, an incarnation of God on earth.

Ram Mohun Roy (c. 1774-1833)

The leader of a movement for the revival and reform of Hindu culture. Ram Mohun Roy was one of the first modern thinkers to form a bridge between the East and West. He learned about Western culture while working for the British East India Company. He also had a deep knowledge of his own culture and translated many of the sacred texts from Sanskrit into Bengali, Hindi and English. He formed a society called the Brahmo Samaj. It stressed Hindu culture but wanted to see the end of some aspects of Hindu life such as the caste system and the ritual death of widows on their husband's funeral pyre. The widow who died in this way was called a "*sati*" or "virtuous woman". The efforts of the Brahmo Samaj helped to bring about a law prohibiting the custom. The Brahmo Samaj also stressed social service. The society's members were mainly intellectuals and it never had a large following. However, many of its ideas were later taken up by other groups.

Ram Mohun Roy died on a visit to England and is buried in Arno Vale cemetery in Bristol.

Ram Mohun Roy, a prominent citizen of Bengal and founder of the Brahmo Samaj, whose members worked for Hindu reform.

Rebirth

Every religion attempts to answer the question "What happens after death?" Hinduism's answer is that the soul is reborn. The cycle of birth and death is called *samsara*. The form that the soul will take in its next life – whether bird, animal or human – is determined by one's actions in this life. This chain of cause and effect is called the law of *karma*.

Explaining rebirth, the *Bhagavad Gita* says:

As a man puts off his worn out clothes
    and puts on other new ones,
so the embodied [soul] puts off worn out bodies
    and goes to others that are new.

Rig Veda

One of Hinduism's oldest and most sacred books. The *Rig Veda* contains 1,028 hymns in the Sanskrit language. It was probably in use in its present form by around 900 BC. This makes it the oldest religious text in the world which is still in use and still considered sacred.

The hymns of the *Rig Veda* were chanted at the ancient Aryan fire sacrifice. They were handed down orally for centuries before they were written down. The hymns are still chanted today at marriages and funerals and in daily rituals.

46

Sacred books

Hinduism has no single sacred book, such as the Bible in Christianity or the Qur'an in Islam. Instead, there are many religious books, written at different times. It is difficult to assign dates to Hinduism's sacred books. Many were compiled gradually over the centuries and contain some very ancient parts as well as others that are more recent. Many were handed down orally for centuries before they were written down. Among the most important of Hinduism's sacred books are the:

Four Vedas The oldest and most sacred is the *Rig Veda*, a collection of hymns probably in use by 900 BC. The others are the *Sama Veda*, *Yajur Veda* and *Atharva Veda*.

Brahmanas Commentaries on the *Vedas*, written mainly from 900-700 BC.

Upanishads Great mystical texts written around 700-500 BC.

Dharma Sutras Guidelines for good conduct, providing the earliest view of Hindu law. Probably composed between 600-200 BC, though some parts are much older.

Mahabharata The great epic telling of the war between the Pandavas and Kauravas. The most important section, the *Bhagavad Gita*, is sometimes called the "Hindu Bible" because of its great popularity. The *Mahabharata* was in use in its present form in the early centuries AD.

Ramayana The great epic telling the story of Prince Rama of Ayodhya, the seventh *avatar* of Vishnu. The Sanskrit version by Valmiki was probably written sometime between 200 BC and 200 AD. The popular version by Tulsi Das in Hindi was written in the seventeenth century.

Dharma Shastras Ancient law books, including the *Laws of Manu*. Some sections are based on the earlier *Dharma Sutras*. The *Laws of Manu* were probably in use in their present form in around 100-200 AD.

Puranas Collections of ancient stories about the gods and goddesses. Written down in their present form at various times from 400 AD or earlier to 1000 AD or later.

Bhakti hymns Written by various devotees, often in the everyday language of the worshipper rather than Sanskrit. The hymns stress the worshipper's love of god and the love that god returns. *Bhakti* hymns were probably sung in temples by around 500 AD and are still being written and sung today.

Sacred thread

A loop of thread worn over the left shoulder and under the right arm. The sacred thread is worn only by men, and only by those of the top three classes – Brahmins, Kshatriyas and Vaishyas. The sacred thread ceremony is considered a second birth, and those who wear the thread are called the twice born.

The sacred thread ceremony can be held at any time from the age of nine onward. Traditionally, the ceremony marked the time when a boy became a full member of the community. He could then learn more about the sacred books and rituals, some of which were known only to the twice born.

Today, the sacred thread is worn more often by Brahmins than by other groups.

A special ceremony held each year at which the sacred thread can be changed for a new one. These men have gathered to bathe in the sea near Bombay and then perform the ceremony to take a new sacred thread. The priest performing the ceremony is near the back reading from a sacred book.

Sadhu

A holy man or saint, an ascetic. Most Hindus lead ordinary lives, earning a living and bringing up their families. A few, however, decide to give up everything to search for spiritual truth. A *sadhu* may go to the mountains alone to meditate or he may wander from one sacred place of pilgrimage to another. *Sadhus* often travel long distances on foot, stopping at villages to rest. The villagers provide the *sadhu* with food, and in return he usually speaks to them on religious subjects. Most *sadhus* are men. It is generally considered inappropriate for a woman to become a wandering ascetic.

A *sadhu* or holy man, garlanded with flowers and carrying all of his belongings with him. The dish in his hand is used to beg for food. In Hinduism it is generally felt that one gains religious merit by giving food to such holy men. Young men may become *sadhus*, but often wandering holy men are old men who have given up their homes to enter the fourth stage of life. Those who have entered the fourth stage of life are called *sannyasis*. (See *Ashramas*.)

Samsara

The cycle of birth and death. (See *Rebirth*.)

Sannyasi

A holy man. A homeless, wandering ascetic. A person who has entered the fourth stage of life, leaving his home and giving up all of his possessions to search for spiritual truth. (See *Ashramas*.)

Sanskrit

The language of ancient India in which many of the sacred books of Hinduism are written. Sanskrit is one of the ancient tongues in the family of Indo-European languages, along with Latin and Greek. In some words the relationship is easy to see. For instance, *devas*, which means "gods" in Sanskrit, is related to the Latin *deus* and the modern English word "divine". *Raja*, meaning "king", is related to the Latin *rex* and English "regal". *Agni*, meaning "fire", is related to the Latin *ignis* and English "ignite". *Matr* and *pitr* in Sanskrit are, of course, "mother" and "father".

Most modern North Indian languages are derived from Sanskrit. These include Hindi, Gujarati, Bengali, Punjabi, etc. Though Sanskrit is no longer spoken, it is still used for religious ceremonies.

A verse from the *Rig Veda* written in Sanskrit, the language of ancient India. The verse, called the Gayatri, is an especially important one and is recited each day by many Hindus. The verse here begins with an invocation and then reads: "Let us think on the lovely splendour of the god Saviter that he may inspire our minds."

ॐ
भूर्भुवस्सुवः
तत् सवितुर्वरेण्यं
भर्गो देवस्य धीमहि
धियो योनः प्रचोदयात्

Saraswati

The goddess of art, music and learning, and the wife of the god Brahma. Saraswati is pictured as a beautiful woman, who carries a *veena* (a stringed musical instrument) and a book. Her vehicle is either a peacock or a swan. As the goddess of learning, Saraswati is particularly important to students. She is also the special goddess of writers, musicians and artists.

Saraswati is said to have invented the Sanskrit language and the *Devanagari* script in which it is written.

At one time Saraswati was a river goddess, like Ganga. In the *Rig Veda*, the Saraswati river is described as flowing from the mountains as far as the sea. It is praised for bringing fertility to the soil and for the purifying power of its waters. The goddess Saraswati is said to bring fertility, fatness and wealth.

Over the centuries, the river has dried up. It is now a small stream that disappears in the Rajasthan desert. However, Saraswati is still associated with a river. Some say the river Saraswati now flows underground and that it joins the Ganges and Jamuna rivers near the city of Allahabad. The place where the Ganges and Jamuna rivers meet is considered a particularly holy spot.

The beautiful goddess Saraswati playing the *veena*.

49

Science and mathematics

At the time of the fall of the Roman empire, when Europe was entering the "Dark Ages", Hindu scientists and mathematicians were enjoying an era of brilliant discoveries. India was at this time ruled by the great Gupta kings. The Gupta period, sometimes called the golden age of Hindu art and culture, was a time when the sciences flourished as well.

Calculations in Gupta India were done with the decimal system of numbers now used in the West, with nine digits and a zero. The system was invented and developed in India. It was passed on to the West by the Arabs, freeing European mathematicians from the cumbersome system of Roman numerals.

Ancient Indian mathematicians developed a form of algebra, knew the importance of positive and negative numbers, calculated square roots, and worked out the value of *pi* at 3.1416. They also wrote about the larger implications of zero and infinity. Perhaps Hindu ideas of infinite space and the cyclical nature of time opened the doors to higher mathematics.

Astronomers at the Gupta court knew of seven planets and charted their movements quite accurately, though they did not have the telescope. They knew the cause of eclipses and were able to forecast them. They also knew that the earth was round and not flat. The fifth-century astronomer and mathematician Aryabhata suggested that the earth revolved around the sun and rotated on its axis. The seventh-century scientist Brahmagupta calculated the circumference of the earth with reasonable accuracy.

It should be noted, however, that many less scientific ideas were also held at this time. The *Puranas* and other sacred texts describe a flat earth. In some books it is said to be made up of seven continents surrounded by seven seas – of salt water, treacle, wine, ghee, milk, curds and fresh water. For some people these "treacle and milk seas" were purely imaginary and belonged to the world of myth. Others, it seems, felt they were real. Thus, great scientific discoveries and fantastic ideas were both put forward. Scientists were not persecuted for revolutionary thinking. Instead, Hinduism, in its all-embracing way, did not reject one or the other. Various levels of thought were allowed to exist side by side.

Other areas of science also flourished in Gupta times. In the field of medicine, for instance, drugs **were** made from herbs and other plants as well as **minerals**. Doctors were able to set broken bones,

The Janter Manter observatory built in Delhi by Maharaja Jai Singh II in around 1724. Jai Singh II took a special interest in astronomy and had five such observatory parks built in North India.

deliver babies by Caesarian section when necessary and carry out plastic surgery to repair wounds received in battle. Several ancient books on medicine have survived, showing that they also knew the importance of cleanliness, light and fresh air.

Some of the most interesting scientific theories were developed long before Gupta times. By around 500 BC – the time the Buddha was living and teaching – an atomic theory was suggested. Atoms were seen as the smallest objects capable of occupying space. It was thought that these combined · together to form larger structures, similar to molecules. Atoms were generally thought to be made up of four elements: earth, air, fire and water. The atomic theory was developed by people trying to figure out what matter was made of. They had no way of carrying out scientific experiments.

Also by 500 BC it was felt that there were tiny creatures living in the air and water, too small to be seen with the naked eye. The microscope was not invented until some 2,000 years later.

After the age of the Guptas, scientific development declined in India. Invasions destroyed the wealth and stability of court life. By the time the industrial revolution was taking place in the West, there seem to have been few opportunities for scientists in India. The rulers do not seem to have been interested in systematically supporting scientific research and scientists seem to have lost some of their spark and confidence.

Today, the field of science in India is full of contradictions. India is a developing country. Many people have a low standard of living. The money that is needed for scientific research is often not available. Still, India has made great scientific advances. It is, for instance, a member of the "nuclear club" with great nuclear research centres. It has also built and launched its own communications satellites. Each year, however, hundreds of Indian scientists move to Western countries where there is more money and better facilities. The "brain drain" has become one of the greatest problems for science in India. Thus, at the present time, some great Hindu scientists can be found working in India, but others have found jobs in the laboratories and universities of countries such as the USA, Britain and West Germany.

Shakti

Female power or energy, personified by the goddess. For some Hindus the god is aloof, while his *shakti* or wife is active in the world. The god is best approached through his *shakti*. The male and female forces of the world are sometimes represented by Shiva and his *shakti*.

Shankara (c. 788-c. 820)

(also known as Shankaracharya) A great Hindu philosopher. Shankara is one of the most famous exponents of the Vedanta school of Hindu philosophy, stressing the importance of the *Upanishads*. Because of his emphasis on the One-ness of the World Spirit, Shankara's teachings are often called "monist". They are also called *advaita*, which means "non-dual" – another way of saying the same thing.

Shankara was born in a village in South India. He was a Brahmin and his family were devotees of the god Shiva. Shankara's father died while he was a child. While still a youth, Shankara decided to break all worldly ties and to seek spiritual truth. He left his mother and travelled north to Banaras, an important centre of Hindu learning. After studying there for several years, he travelled throughout India, teaching and debating with his opponents. During his travels, he founded a number of monasteries, several of which are still thriving today. Shankara wrote commentaries on the *Upanishads* and other sacred books. His thinking has provided the basis for much of modern Hindu philosophy.

Shanti

The Sanskrit word for "peace".

SHIVA

Shiva

One of Hinduism's most important gods. Most
Hindus belong to one of three main sects: those
who worship Shiva as the main god, those who
worship Vishnu as the main god and those who
worship the goddess as the main deity. Some
sacred books speak of the three most important
gods as Brahma, the creator; Vishnu, the
preserver; and Shiva, the destroyer. However,
today few people worship Brahma as a main god.
For most worshippers of Shiva and Vishnu, both
these gods have the power to create and destroy.

Shiva is a fascinating god of great power and
complexity. He is a great ascetic and yogi (a person
who practises yoga) and is the special god of holy
men or *sadhus*. He is often pictured meditating,
high in the Himalaya mountains. He sits on an
animal skin, with legs crossed in the lotus posture
of yoga. His weapon, the trident, and his begging
bowl are placed nearby. Like the holy men of
India, he has his hair matted and piled high on his
head and his body smeared with ashes. He wears
only the skin of a tiger or elephant wrapped round
his waist. Snakes wind their way round his chest
and arms. Once, when he was in deep meditation,
Kama, the god of love, dared to try to tempt him.
Shiva briefly opened the third eye in the centre of
his forehead and burnt him to a cinder. Shiva's
third eye is usually shown in statues and pictures of
him.

Shiva is often pictured with the goddess Ganga
in his hair. According to one story, when the River
Ganga (Ganges) descended from heaven to earth, it
was feared that the crashing force of the water
would destroy the world. Shiva allowed the Ganga
to flow through his long hair to break her fall.
Thus, he wears the river itself or the river goddess
in his matted locks.

In some pictures Shiva is shown with a purple
spot on his neck. This resulted from his swallowing
poison so powerful that it would have destroyed
any of the other gods. It lodged in Shiva's throat,
turning the spot purple.

Sometimes this great god is pictured as Shiva
Nataraja, Lord of the Dance. There are many
beautiful South Indian bronze statues of him
dancing in a circle of flame. Like most Indian art,
these statues are symbolic in many ways, holding a
deeper meaning than first meets the eye. The circle
of flame, for instance, serves as a kind of halo but
also represents the cycle of time, which has no
beginning and no end. Shiva dances on the dwarf
of ignorance, which he destroys for the good of the
world. He has four arms – more than ordinary

Shiva as Lord of the Dance or Shiva Nataraja. He
dances in a circle of flame, treading the dwarf of
ignorance under foot. A small figure of the goddess
Ganga can be seen on the right, in the flowing locks
of Shiva's hair.

Shiva is often worshipped in the form of the *linga*. Here a *linga* stands at the water's edge, with several smaller *linga* in front of it. Shiva's vehicle, the bull Nandi, faces the *lingas*.

human beings – because he has more powers. One hand holds a small drum with which he beats out the rhythm of his dance. Another holds a flame, symbolizing his power to destroy. The third hand gives a blessing and the fourth points to his feet, for it is at the feet of Shiva that devotees can find happiness and refuge.

Shiva's dancing is often said to represent the energy that drives the universe. It was the energy of Shiva's dance that created the world, it flows through it and preserves it, and it will be the fierce energy of Shiva's wild dancing that will destroy the world. And then Shiva will begin to dance again, and the world will be re-created. The cycle will be repeated over and over, endlessly through time.

Shiva is also the god of creation and as such is represented by the *linga*, a rounded pillar. The *linga* represents both the masculine creative forces of the universe and the ancient idea of the central pillar or *axis mundi* separating heaven and earth.

Shiva's wife is the goddess Parvati, also known as Durga or Kali. His vehicle is Nandi, the bull. In many Shiva temples a special shrine is built for Nandi outside the main temple. It usually faces the main image in the temple so that Nandi can always gaze upon his Lord. For this reason, statues of Nandi usually have a blissful smile.

Shruti and Smriti

The sacred books of Hinduism are divided into two groups, *shruti* (heard) and *smriti* (remembered). Those classed as *shruti*, the word revealed by God, are the more sacred. These include the *Vedas* and *Upanishads*. The later works are all *smriti*. These include the epics, the *Puranas* and the law books.

Shudra

The lowest of the four classes or *varna*. Traditionally, it was the role of the *Shudra* to serve the three higher classes.

Sita

The wife of the god Rama. For many Hindus, Sita is considered the ideal wife – beautiful, devoted, pure and tender.

In the *Ramayana*, Sita happily goes with Rama into exile in the forest. There she is captured by the demon king Ravana who carries her off to his palace in Lanka. Ravana makes many efforts to win her, but Sita remains true to Rama. Finally, with the help of Hanuman and his army of monkeys, Rama rescues Sita.

The ending of the *Ramayana* seems harsh on Sita to many readers. Once she is safe, Rama begins to have doubts. After all, she has lived under the roof of another man, he reasons. Sita proves her purity by asking that a funeral pyre be built. She then enters the fire, but it does not burn her. Rama accepts this proof, but when they return home to the kingdom of Ayodhya (the fourteen years they were to wander in the forest has now ended) people begin to whisper and gossip about Sita. Rama unhappily sends her out of the kingdom to please his people, and she goes to live in a hermitage in the forest. Finally, at the end of the *Ramayana*, she asks the earth to swallow her up. The earth opens and Sita disappears.

Sita, the devoted wife of the god Rama, beside him on a throne. Rama's loyal brother Lakshman stands behind them, while Hanuman, the humble monkey god, touches Rama's foot.

Soma

A sacred drink that worshippers shared at some Vedic rituals. The drink seems to have caused a feeling of great happiness and elation. For unknown reasons, the drinking of *soma* was dropped from Vedic rituals at an early date. No one is sure what the drink was made of. Some scholars think it was made of hemp, the plant which is the source of drugs such as marijuana. The drink was sometimes personified as the god Soma. There are a number of hymns to Soma in the *Rig Veda*.

Stages of Life

See *Ashramas*.

Temples

Visits to a temple are an important part of religion for most Hindus. However, there are no set rules stating when or how often a person should go to the temple. There is no weekly congregational gathering such as the Sunday service of Christianity or prayers at the mosque on Friday for Muslims. A person can go to the temple once a week, once a month or never at all and still be a good Hindu.

When people go to the temple, they usually go alone or in small family groups. Offerings of food or flowers are usually taken. Most temples have one or several bells at the gateway that worshippers ring as they enter. Once inside, the worshipper may stop at several small shrines to offer prayers before going to the main shrine. A temple priest usually sits near the main shrine. The offerings of food or flowers are given to him, and he places them before the statue of the god or goddess. The worshipper may then walk around the image as a sign of reverence and offer prayers. The priest makes a red mark called a *tilak* on the worshipper's forehead with red kum kum powder and rice grains. Some of the food offered to the god is given back to the worshipper by the priest. Other food, especially sweets from the temple, are also given to the worshipper. Food received from the temple is called *prashad*, which means "grace". In taking it, the devotee accepts the blessing of the god. The food is shared with family or friends or given to the poor. *Prashad* should never be wasted or handled disrespectfully.

The type of worship described above is called *puja*. Sometimes the *puja* at a temple may be much more elaborate. Several priests may take part and offerings of various sorts might be made. *Arti* is often performed as part of the *puja*. Sometimes, however, *puja* can be even simpler. For instance, an office worker might stop at a roadside shrine on his way to work, place a few flowers on the altar, offer prayers and carry on on his way.

India is often called a land of temples, but at one time temples were not an important part of worship. The Aryans carried out most of their ceremonies before a simple fire altar made of brick. There was probably no image of a god or goddess. The Aryans were a nomadic people, moving from place to place with their herds of cattle. The fire altar could be easily put together at a new site.

It is thought that the earliest temples were probably built of brick and wood. By 300 AD temples were regularly used for worship, though few from this time have survived. Among the

A gateway (or *gopuram*) of the Meenakshi temple in the city of Madurai, Tamil Nadu. Many South Indian temples have elaborate gateways like this one. Sometimes the gateways are more impressive than the temple itself.

The Lakshmana temple at Khajuraho, built in around 1000 AD. The towers are in the Northern style and each is topped with a water pot, symbol of abundance. The temple is made of stone and covered with beautiful carvings.

earliest surviving temples are cave temples. These were carved by hand from solid rock. There are often a number of cave temples, one next to the other, stretching along a hillside. One of the finest groups of Hindu cave temples is located at Ellora, 200 kilometres from Bombay. Some 30 cave temples were made here between the fifth and eighth centuries AD. One of the finest is the Kailashanatha temple, dedicated to the great god Shiva. It is different from the other cave temples in that the entire hillside has been carved away to leave a stone building. It is about the size of the Parthenon of ancient Greece and is covered with beautiful stone sculpture.

The earliest existing free-standing stone temples date back to around the sixth century AD. Two main styles of temple building developed in India, known as the Northern and Southern styles. They are similar in many ways. In both, the most sacred part of the temple, where the icon of the god or goddess stands, is a small, dark chamber. In front of the chamber are one or several halls, with beautifully carved pillars. At the entrance, there is often a covered porch.

A tall tower rises directly over the spot where the

sacred icon stands. The shape of the tower is one of the main differences between the Northern and Southern styles. In the North the tower rises straight up and then slopes gently inward. In the South it is more like a great four-sided pyramid. In both styles, the top of the temple is usually crowned with one or several water pots, a symbol of abundance.

Hindu temples are generally very lively buildings, covered inside and outside with carvings of plants and animals as well as of people and gods. The elephants seem to prance, the women dance, and even the plants twist and bend, creating the feeling that the whole building is bursting with life.

Near the main temple there may be several smaller shrines as well as other structures, such as housing for the temple priests. The whole complex is usually surrounded by a wall, to mark off the sacred area. In the South the wall was given greater importance. Here some temples have several high walls, one inside the other, with soaring gateways.

Most temples are built near water, so that worshippers can bathe to purify themselves before entering the temple. Many are built along rivers. Some temples have great sunken tanks filled with water.

Instructions for building temples are contained in ancient textbooks (*silpashastras*). These guidelines are still followed by modern temple builders, who combine traditional ideas with modern building techniques and styles.

Time

In Hindu thought, time has no beginning and no end, but moves in great cycles. The universe is created, it prospers, it then declines and is destroyed – and then it is created again. This happens over and over, endlessly.

After the universe is created, it passes through four eras called *yugas*. The names of the *yugas* are *krita*, *treta*, *dvapara* and *kali*. The first *yuga* is the best. It is a golden age when there is only goodness in the world. In each of the following ages, things get progressively worse. We are now in the *kali yuga*, the worst of all times. It is the shortest of the four *yugas* and will last in all some 432,000 years.

Hinduism's cosmic calculations cover extremely long periods. Each cycle of four *yugas* is called a *mahayuga*. Two thousand *mahayugas* make a *kalpa* – some 4,320,000,000 years.

Tolerance

Hindus are generally proud of the tolerance of their faith. At the very core of Hinduism is the idea that many paths – not just one – lead to the Truth. Hinduism itself is a varied religion which offers its followers several different paths. A Hindu may feel that the one he or she has chosen is best, but will usually acknowledge that there are also other ways to find God.

This idea has been expressed in many ways. In the *Bhagavad Gita*, Krishna says:

> In any way that men love me in that same way they find my love: for many are the paths of men, but they all in the end come to me.

The saint and poet Rajjab, who lived some 400 years ago, wrote:

The worship of different sects, which are like so many small streams, move together to meet God, who is like the Ocean.

Mahatma Gandhi said:

> I came to the conclusion long ago . . . that all religions are true and, also, that all had some error in them; and that whilst I hold my own, I should hold others as dear as Hinduism; . . . . So, we can only pray, if we are Hindus, not that a Christian should become a Hindu; or if we are Mussulmans [Muslims], not that a Hindu or a Christian should become a Mussulman; nor should we ever secretly pray that anyone should be converted; but our inward prayer should be that a Hindu should be a better Hindu, a Muslim a better Muslim and a Christian a better Christian.

Twice born

The sacred thread ceremony is considered a second birth and those who wear the sacred thread are called "twice born". (See *Sacred thread*.)

Untouchables

Those outside the four social classes or *varna*. Traditionally, the Untouchables did all the worst jobs, which the higher classes considered polluting. For example, they washed the clothes of the higher classes, cleaned their homes, swept the streets and hauled away the bodies of dead animals. Untouchables often lived in hovels some distance away from the other villagers. They were usually the poorest group in the village and were dependent on the upper classes for their jobs and livelihood.

Contact with an Untouchable was considered

polluting. If a Brahmin accidentally touched an Untouchable, he or she would bathe and perform special rituals to become pure again. This is often still the case, though Gandhi and many other Hindus fought to end Untouchability. Gandhi spoke of the "miserable, wretched, enslaving spirit of 'untouchableness'", which he said was a blot on Hinduism. He called the Untouchables "*Harijans*" or "Children of God". When India gained its independence, Untouchability was outlawed in the Indian Constitution.

Today, many more children from low caste and formerly Untouchable communities are receiving a good education. In villages, low caste groups are beginning to demand their rights as equal citizens and to use the power of the vote to improve their position. Many low caste villagers have moved to the city to become bus drivers and office clerks and thus escape their traditional role. Places in universities are set aside for members of castes that were considered Untouchable, special scholarships are available and several seats in Parliament are set aside for members of disadvantaged castes. But old ideas about Untouchability have been slow to die among some groups of Hindus, and laws prohibiting discrimination have proved difficult to enforce. Poverty and prejudice are still the lot of many ex-Untouchables.

A sweeper at his work. Although the Indian constitution outlaws Untouchability, many caste Hindus would still consider this man to be an Untouchable.

Upanishads

Great mystical books, which are among Hinduism's most sacred texts. The *Upanishads* date back to around 700-500 BC. They show a new direction in ancient Indian thought. Ideas such as rebirth, *karma* and *moksha* are stressed for the first time in the *Upanishads*. A main theme is the nature of the World Soul (*Brahman*) and the individual soul (*Atman*). The ideas of the *Upanishads* were also important for the new religions of Buddhism and Jainism, which were being taught by the Buddha and Mahavira in about 500 BC.

The *Upanishads* were among the first of Hinduism's holy books to be translated into English, German and other Western languages. Their power and beauty inspired many people, including poets, philosophers and artists. Although Hinduism is a religion of many levels, people in the West often think of it mainly as a great mystical religion. This is due, in part, to the impact the *Upanishads* made.

The best way to understand the *Upanishads* is, of course, to read them. There are a number of good English translations. A small part of the wisdom of the *Upanishads* is summed up in the short excerpts here:

There is a Spirit which is pure and which is beyond old age and death; and beyond hunger and thirst and sorrow. This is Atman, the spirit in man. All the desires of the Spirit are Truth. It is this Spirit that we must find and know: Man must find his own Soul. He who has found and knows his Soul has found all the worlds, has achieved all his desires. (*Chandogya Upanishad*)

From delusion lead me to Truth.
From darkness lead me to Light.
From death lead me to immortality.
(*Brihad-Aranyaka Upanishad*)

Vahana

A vehicle. Every Hindu deity has an animal (or part animal) vehicle on which he or she rides. Shiva's vehicle or *vahana* is the bull, Nandi. Vishnu's is the Garuda, an eagle-like bird, sometimes pictured as half man and half bird.

Vaishya

The third of the four social classes or *varna*. Traditionally, Vaishyas were merchants, traders and businessmen.

Varna

Hindu society is divided into four classes or *varna*: Brahmins (priests and teachers), Kshatriyas (rulers and warriors), Vaishyas (traders and businessmen) and Shudras (workers who serve the other three classes).

The four classes date back some 3000 years to the early days of Aryan settlement in India. A hymn in the *Rig Veda* describes the creation of the four *varna* from a primeval man. It says:

The Brahmin was his mouth,
  of his arms was made the warrior,
his thighs became the Vaishya,
  of his feet the Shudra was born.

It is likely that when the Aryans came to India they already had a three-level social structure made up of priests, warriors and ordinary members of the tribe. The Shudra class may have been added later to include the local people of India, whom the Aryans dominated. It seems these social divisions became more strict and rigid with time. Also a fifth group was added. These were the Untouchables who formed the lowest level of society and were outside the *varna* system altogether.

The word *varna* means colour. It is possible that the class divisions were based to some extent on skin colour. Thus, the lighter-skinned Aryans made up the top three classes, while the darker-skinned local people became the Shudras and Untouchables.

The *varna* system continues to be important today. Every Hindu belongs to one of the four *varna* – or else is an Untouchable. However, many people no longer perform the social function assigned to their *varna*. Brahmins, for instance, are not all priests and Kshatriyas do a variety of jobs.

The *varna* system remains important mainly in terms of caste ranking. It is estimated that there are some 2,000 small caste groups or *jati* in India. Some extend only over one area or region. But each of these claims membership in one of the *varna* groups. Thus, the four *varna* provide an India-wide framework into which the many smaller caste groups fit. (For further details, see *Caste*.)

Varnashrama dharma

The code of conduct based on a person's class (*varna*) and stage of life (*ashrama*). There is a general *dharma* or social code that applies to everyone. All people should be truthful, kind, just, loyal, etc. However, at the same time, there are also different codes for different people, based on class and stage of life. What is right for a Brahmin is not necessarily right for a Shudra; and what is right for an old man is not necessarily right for a student. (For further details, see *Dharma*, as well as *Varna* and *Ashrama*.)

Vedas

Ancient sacred books. The *Rig Veda, Sama Veda, Yajur Veda* and *Atharva Veda* make up the four *Vedas*. By far the oldest and most sacred is the *Rig Veda*, a collection of 1,028 hymns. The *Rig Veda* was in use in its present form by around 900 BC, though some parts may date back as far as 1500 BC. The hymns were recited during the Aryan fire sacrifice.

The *Sama Veda* contains hymns from the *Rig Veda* arranged in a different order, for use in various ceremonies. The *Yajur Veda* is made up of instructions for the priest performing the sacrifice, with phrases to be recited by him. The *Atharva Veda* contains magical spells as well as hymns to the gods.

The *Vedas* are in the Sanskrit language. They were passed down orally for hundreds of years before they were finally written down. Hymns from the *Vedas* are still recited in Sanskrit at rites such as marriages and funerals.

Village Hinduism

Hinduism is a religion that can be practised on many different levels. Over 75% of the population of India lives in villages. Here the great Sanskrit books and the schools of philosophy are not very important in everyday life. What is important can vary enormously. From the North to the South of India and from the East to the West villages are very different. People eat different kinds of food, wear different styles of clothes, speak different languages, live in different sorts of houses and practise Hinduism in many different ways. Some generalizations can be made about village Hinduism, but there will always be many exceptions.

In general, the basic beliefs of Hinduism are well-known at the village level. Rebirth and *karma* are as familiar to the villager as they are to the city dweller. Caste is more important in the village. Traditionally, the caste system provided a job and a role for everyone. The potter's son became a potter and the carpenter's son a carpenter, giving great stability to village life. This is still true to a large extent.

The great gods Shiva and Vishnu are known and are worshipped in the village. There are also many local gods that vary from one village to another. A wide variety of spirits, ghosts and minor gods also have a place in village religion. Offerings are made to them with the main aim of keeping them content and happy so that they will not cause problems in the village. When problems do arise, such spirits are often blamed. Amulets and charms are often worn to combat evil spirits.

Most villages have several shrines. Worship is usually the simple *puja*, similar to that in any larger temple. Hymn singing is also an important religious activity. Villagers gather regularly in the evening to sing the praises of various gods. Festivals add colour and variety to village life. Which festivals are celebrated and how they are celebrated vary from village to village. But in all villages, festival celebrations are an important part of religious life.

No matter how remote it is, no Indian village is really cut off from the rest of the world. Villagers travel to nearby markets and towns, and religious ideas flow with trade and travel. Wandering *sadhus* or holy men visit the village, and the villagers

Villagers outside a building with pictures of the goddess Durga and the god Shiva. The great gods and goddesses of Hinduism play an important role in the village as well as the city.

gather in the evening to hear their teachings. Pilgrimage has been important in the spread of religious ideas. Groups of villagers often travel great distances to visit the magnificent temples or holy places of Hinduism. There they meet other pilgrims from distant parts of India, and all sit together and listen to the words of holy men and teachers. When they return to the village, they bring with them new myths and stories, new hymns and a deeper understanding of their faith.

Vishnu

One of Hinduism's most important gods. Most Hindus worship either Vishnu, Shiva or the goddess as the main deity.

Vishnu is both a powerful and a kind god. He is in many ways like a good father or a great and just king. He is worshipped with great devotion, but little fear.

Vishnu's appearance is in keeping with his kingly qualities. He wears a tall, jewelled crown and is often pictured seated on a throne. He is usually shown with four arms. As is the case with most Hindu gods, Vishnu's many arms show his many powers. Vishnu carries a lotus, conch shell, discus and club. Vishnu's wife is Lakshmi, the beautiful goddess of wealth and good fortune. Sometimes they are shown riding together on Vishnu's vehicle, the Garuda, an eagle-like creature, often depicted as half man and half bird.

Vishnu is sometimes pictured sleeping on a great hundred-headed serpent called Shesha. In this case, the scene is set for the creation of the world. According to one story, Brahma appears on a lotus that grows from Vishnu's navel while he sleeps. Brahma creates the world and Vishnu awakes to reign over it. After many eras the world is destroyed again. Nothing exists but Vishnu, who sleeps on the serpent Shesha, floating in the ocean of eternity. Then the world is created once more. The story is repeated over and over, through the endless cycle of time.

Vishnu is often worshipped in the form of one of his *avatars* or incarnations. These are forms that Vishnu has taken on earth. Whenever evil gets the upper hand, Vishnu comes to the aid of mankind to set the balance right. Most Hindus recognize nine incarnations in the past – and a tenth that is still to come. By far the most widely worshipped *avatars* are the gods Krishna and Rama. (For further details, see *Avatar, Krishna, Rama.*)

The god Vishnu wearing the tall crown and jewellery of a king. He carries the conch shell in his lower left hand and the discus in his upper left hand. His upper right hand holds a club and his lower right hand makes the gesture of "offering a boon". His vehicle, the Garuda, can be seen at the bottom of the statue.

Vivekananda (1862-1902)

A disciple of the saint Ramakrishna and a great Hindu spiritual leader. Vivekananda founded the Ramakrishna Mission, which has branches throughout the world. In the West the mission is mainly a centre where people can learn about Hinduism and the teachings of Ramakrishna. In India, its members do social work, helping the needy in cities and villages.

Vivekananda was one of the first Indians in modern times to travel abroad and to teach non-Hindus about Hinduism. He attended the World Parliament of Religions in Chicago in 1893, and his message was so captivating that newspapers described him as "undoubtedly the greatest figure at the Parliament". He felt that the West had much to give India in the form of science and industry, and that India had much to offer the West in its ancient religious teachings. Vivekananda lectured in many cities in the USA and UK, stressing the theme of One World combining Western progress and Indian spirituality.

The great religious leader, Swami Vivekananda, was one of the first Hindus to travel to Europe and America to teach about Hinduism.

Women

The roles of women in Hindu society are numerous and varied. In the village, a woman's main work is running the household. Village women are up at the crack of dawn gathering fire wood, fetching water from the well, cooking, cleaning and caring for animals and children. Many women work in the fields as well as in the home. Much of the planting, harvesting and winnowing of grain is done by women. Crafts such as pot-making are handed

Women's roles are varied. Some women work in the fields as well as the home. These women are transplanting rice.

down from father to son, but wives and daughters also help in the work.

Children are an especially important part of women's lives. Almost all Hindu couples hope to have at least one son, who will light his parents' funeral pyres and carry out rites for them after they are dead. A woman who has no children or no son is considered unfortunate.

In towns and cities, many women work in banks, shops, schools or hospitals. Much heavy labour is also done by women. This includes carrying loads of bricks on construction sites and breaking stones to pave the roads. However, a majority of women in cities spend most of their time caring for children and keeping house. Many Indians live in large family groups, often called the joint family. The bride goes to live in her husband's home. Usually, the youngest daughter-in-law has the lowest status in the household and does the most work.

In the home, men appear to have a superior position. Men usually eat their meals together. The women serve them and eat afterwards. Women cover their heads when an older relative enters the room, especially an older male relative. However, it is usually the women who have the most say in the running of the home. They keep the keys to all the cupboards and keep track of spending. In a happy home the women are respected, and it is generally felt that they bring love and dignity to the household.

The sacred books provide some guidelines on women's roles, but these are often contradictory. The conservative *Laws of Manu* say:

> She should do nothing independently even in her own house. In childhood subject to her father, in youth to her husband, and when her husband is dead to her sons, she should never enjoy independence.

However, the *Upanishads* speak of women philosophers who debated with the best male minds of their age. Other books mention women who owned shops and ran businesses and seem to have led very independent lives.

Sita, the wife of the god Rama, is often held up as the ideal Hindu wife – devoted, loyal and ever-willing to serve her husband. However, in the great epic, the *Mahabharata*, the capable Draupadi is married to all five of the Pandava brothers and manages her five husbands quite well.

Thus, on the subject of women, as in most other areas, Hinduism is a diverse religion. India is a country where most women lead traditional lives, either because they want to or because social pressures force them to. But it is also a country that has produced great women leaders. The Rani of Jhansi, for instance, led her troops against the British in the Rebellion of 1857. After several stunning victories she was killed in battle. In recent times Indira Gandhi has been one of the world's few women Prime Ministers.

... These girls, on the other hand, are getting an education. They may have a career or a traditional life at home.

Worship

In Hinduism, worship can take many forms. The most frequent is *puja*. This can be a simple rite, where flowers or food are presented to a deity and prayers offered, or an elaborate ritual. *Puja* is performed both in the home and at the temple. (For further details, see *Puja, Family shrine* and *Temple*.)

Another, less frequent, type of worship is *yajna*, the Vedic sacrifice. *Yajna* is performed before the sacred fire. Offerings are made to the gods of ghee

Worship in a Hindu temple in Glasgow, UK. The ceremony is taking place round the sacred fire, with offerings of food such as ghee and rice placed in its flames.

and other foods, placed in the fire. One or several Brahmin priests perform *yajna* rites.

Along with these two kinds of worship there are many others. Prayer beads are sometimes used. A person may sit in a quiet place and repeat the names of God, counting them off on the beads. Meditation, reading from the sacred books and hymn singing are all forms of worship, as is pilgrimage to the sacred places of Hinduism. Giving alms to the poor, helping those in need, caring for animals that are sick or injured and selflessly serving one's fellow human beings are all ways of worshipping God. In fact, in the *Bhagavad Gita*, Krishna says that a person's life should be a continuous act of worship.

Yantra

A geometrical drawing used to focus concentration in meditation. Both Hindus and Buddhists use *yantras* in meditation.

Yoga

Physical and mental exercises aimed at gaining control of the mind and body. Yoga today has two somewhat different roles. For some, it is a strict spiritual discipline. For others, it is simply good exercise and a way to better health.

For those who practise yoga for purely spiritual reasons, the aim is to achieve *moksha* – liberation, enlightenment, escape from the cycle of birth and death. This may take years of effort, or may never be achieved at all in this lifetime. Yoga has been practised as a spiritual discipline in India for several thousand years. A person who practises yoga is called a *yogi* (male) or *yogini* (female). The ancient books set out a number of requirements for the *yogi* or *yogini*. These include self-control, non-violence, truthfulness, chastity and avoidance of greed. Certain postures, called *asanas*, must also be mastered. The most well-known is the lotus posture or *padma asana*. Here the person sits with legs crossed so that the feet rest on the thighs. Breathing exercises are also important. To aid concentration, the mind may be focused on a statue of a deity or a special diagram called a *yantra*. These are especially designed to lead the mind inward. Word formulas called *mantras* may be repeated over and over. Repeating a *mantra* is said to raise the level of concentration and aid meditation.

Many *yogis* and *yoginis* have been able to perform surprising physical feats. They have learned to withstand pain and to control their breathing and heart-beat rate. Some are also said to gain magical powers. These are hard to test, but continue to hold great fascination.

A far greater number of people practise yoga simply for better health. In recent years, hundreds of yoga schools have opened in Europe and America. These mainly teach the various postures or *asanas*, though some teach meditation as well. Many of those who practise yoga say it is good exercise which brings better health, improved concentration, inner peace and general physical and mental well-being.

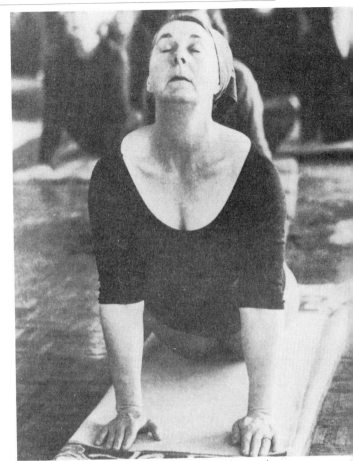

A yoga class in Europe. Yoga has spread beyond the borders of India and is practised all over the world for better health and greater spiritual harmony.

Some Important Dates in the History of Hinduism and India

2000BC	Indus valley cities thriving.
1500	Aryan tribes migrate into India.
900	*Rig Veda* in use for religious ceremonies.
800	Later *Vedas* in use, as well as *Brahmanas*.
700	Early *Upanishads* composed.
c.480	Death of the Buddha, who founded the new religion of Buddhism.
c.468	Death of Mahavira, who taught the religion of Jainism.
326	Alexander the Great leads his army into northwest India.
321	Chandragupta Maurya founds the first great Indian empire (the Mauryan empire).
268-31	The great king Ashoka rules the Mauryan empire, which stretches over most of the Indian subcontinent. Ashoka becomes a follower of Buddhism and India's first great Buddhist king.
200	Early versions of the great religious epics the *Ramayana* and *Mahabharata* are in use. Some parts of these are much older and had been passed on orally for centuries.
100	The *Bhagavad Gita*, a part of the *Mahabharata* and today one of Hinduism's most sacred texts, is in use.
0	Tribes from Central Asia invade and rule much of northwest India. Their kings adopt Hinduism and Buddhism.
100AD	The *Laws of Manu*, an early Hindu legal code, is in use.
320	The Gupta empire is founded by Chandra Gupta I. The empire flourishes for some 200 years. A "golden age" of Indian culture is attained under the Guptas. Beautiful stone temples are built, sculpture and painting flourish, the great poet and playwright Kali Das composes the classics of Sanskrit literature. Great mathematicians and astronomers such as Aryabhata and Varahamihira make new discoveries. Aryabhata, for instance, suggests that the earth is round, rotates on its axis and revolves around the sun.
400	Some *Puranas* (collections of ancient stories) are in use in their present form. Others may date from 100 AD or later.
606-47	Rule of the great king Harsha.
700	The Pallava dynasty rules much of South India. The Pallava kings encourage the spread of Aryan ideas to South India.
c.820	Death of the great Hindu philosopher Shankara.
900	The Chola dynasty rules much of South India. Great Hindu temples are built. Bronze casting reaches a new level of excellence and beautiful bronze statues of gods and goddesses are made.

1000	Mahmud of Ghazni, a Muslim Turk, launches raids from present-day Afghanistan into North India, carrying back rich pillage.
1137	Death of the great Hindu philosopher Ramanuja.
1200	The Muslim Muhammad Ghurid conquers much of North India and establishes a large empire which breaks up on his death. Independent Muslim sultanates are then established in various parts of India. Islam becomes an important religion in India and wins some converts.
1288	Marco Polo visits South India on his return journey from China.
1469	Birth of Guru Nanak, founder of the Sikh religion.
1498	Vasco da Gama, the Portuguese explorer and trader, arrives in India.
1526	The Mughal empire is established by Babur. Muslim culture flourishes at the Mughal court for the next 200 years, though most Indians remain Hindus.
1500	Mira Bai, a Rajput princess and follower of Krishna, writes beautiful devotional hymns.
1600	The British, Dutch and French East India companies compete with the Portuguese for trade concessions in India. In 1757 the British under Clive win the Battle of Plassey and gain control of much of Bengal, gradually extending their power over much of the sub-continent. Christianity becomes an important religion in India, winning some converts.
1623	Death of Tulsi Das, author of the Hindi version of the *Ramayana*.
1833	Death of Ram Mohun Roy, Hindu social reformer.
1857	Members of the army and other groups rise up against the British in the 1857 Rebellion. In 1858 British India is placed directly under the government of the Crown. Queen Victoria is officially proclaimed Empress of India.
1886	Death of the Hindu saint Ramakrishna.
1902	Death of the religious leader Vivekananda, founder of the Ramakrishna mission.
1915	Gandhi returns to India from South Africa to become a great religious and political leader.
1947	India and Pakistan gain independence from Britain.
1962	The Hindu philosopher Sarvepalli Radhakrishnan becomes the President of India, a largely ceremonial office. He remains president until 1967.
1982	Death of Vinoba Bhave, follower of Gandhi, who travelled across India on foot encouraging landowners to give part of their land to the poor.

Books for Further Reading

An Autobiography, The Story of My Experiments with Truth M.K. Gandhi (Gandhi's autobiography was first published in 1948. Various paperback editions are now available.)

Five Religions in the Twentieth Century W. Owen Cole (Hulton Educational, 1981)

The Five Sons of King Pandu (A simplified version of the *Mahabharata*) Elizabeth Seeger (J.M. Dent, 1970)

Gandhi F.W. Rawding (Cambridge University Press, 1980)

Gandhi George Woodcock (Collins/Fontana, 1972)

Gandhi Malcolm Yapp (Harrap, 1977)

Hanuman R. Ramachandran (Adam and Charles Black, 1979)

A Hindu Family in Britain Peter Bridger (REP Pergamon, 1969)

Hindu Stories V.P. (Hemant) Kanitkar (Wayland, 1986)

The Hindu Tradition Lee Smith and Wes Bodin (eds) (Argus Communications, 1978)

The Hindu World Patricia Bahree (Macdonald Educational, 1982)

Hinduism Yorke Crompton (Ward Lock Educational, 1971)

Hinduism V.P. (Hemant) Kanitkar (Wayland, 1985)

Hinduism Paul Younger and Susanna Oommen Younger (Argus Communications, 1978)

The Ramayana Elizabeth Seeger (J.M. Dent, 1969)

The Story of Prince Rama Brian Thompson (Kestrel Books, 1980)

The Story of Rama and Sita Joanna Troughton (Blackie, 1975)

Thinking About Hinduism Eric Sharpe (Lutterworth Educational, 1971)

For older readers

The Bhagavad Gita Juan Mascaro (trans) (Penguin, 1962)

The Concise Encyclopedia of Living Faiths R.C. Zaehner (ed) (Hutchinson, 1959)

Hindu Myths Wendy Doniger O'Flaherty (Penguin, 1975)

Hindu Scriptures R.C. Zaehner (J.M. Dent, 1966)

The Hindu Temple George Michell (Paul Elek, 1977)

The Hindu View of Life S. Radhakrishnan (Unwin Books, 1966)

Hinduism John Hinnells and Eric Sharpe (eds) (Oriel Press, 1972)

Hinduism K.M. Sen (Penguin, 1961)

Hinduism R.C. Zaehner (Oxford University Press, 1966)

Hinduism in England David Bowen (ed) (Bradford College, 1980)

Indian Mythology Veronica Ions (Hamlyn, 1967)

The Religious Experiences of Mankind Ninian Smart (Collins-Fount Paperback, 1969)

Songs of Krsna Deben Bhattacharya (trans) (Samuel Weiser, 1978)

The Upanishads Juan Mascaro (trans) (Penguin, 1965)

Ways to Shiva Joseph Dye (Philadelphia Museum of Art, 1980)

The Wonder That Was India A.L. Basham (Sidgwick & Jackson, 1967; Fontana/Collins paperback, 1971)

World Religions: A Handbook for Teachers W. Owen Cole (ed) (SHAP Working Party on World Religions in Education, 1976. Supplemented by annual SHAP mailings.)

Index

Agni 4
ahimsa 4, 18, 24
Ajanta caves 6
Akbar 6
Airavata 32
Arjun 13, 34, 35
art 5-6, 34, 49, 50
artha 8
Aryabhata 50
Aryans 5, 7, 9, 17, 20, 29, 30, 32, 44, 46, 55, 59
ascetic 8
Ashoka 5
ashram 8
ashramas 8-9, 48, 60
astronomy 50
Atman 9, 12, 15, 37, 58
atomic theory 51
avatar 9-11, 34, 43-44, 45, 62

Balkrishna 11
Banaras 11, 26, 51
beliefs 12
Bhagavad Gita 9, 12-13, 19, 25, 30, 34, 35, 41, 46, 47, 57, 66
bhajans 13
bhakti 13, 14, 18, 34, 41, 45, 47
Bhave, Vinoba 14
boar *avatar* 9, 10
Brahma (creator god) 14-15, 49, 52
brahmacharin 8
Brahmagupta 50
Brahman (World Spirit) 9, 12, 15, 27, 30, 37, 39, 41, 58
Brahmanas (sacred books) 47
Brahmin (priest) 12, 16, 17, 19, 23, 36, 43, 47, 51, 58, 59, 60, 66
Brahmo Samaj 46
bride 36-37, 64
Buddha 4, 6, 10, 11, 30, 31, 51, 58
Buddhism 4, 5, 30, 58, 66

calendar 16, 22
caste 12, 16-18, 23, 30, 36, 59, 60
ceremonies 7, 18-19, 36-37, 47, 48
Christianity 31, 44, 47, 55, 57
clothing 20
cow, sacred 18, 23, 34
cremation 18-19, 26, 40

dance 38-39
death 18-19, 26, 46
devi 14, 19, 21, 27, 33, 40, 44, 51
devotion 12, 13, 14, 18, 34, 37, 39, 41, 45
dharma 8, 12, 19, 60
Dharma Shastras 35, 47
Dharma Sutras 47
dhoti 20, 21, 24
Divali 22, 23
Draupadi 65
Dravidian 20
dress 20-21
Durga 19, 21, 22, 53, 61
Dussehra 22-23
dwarf *avatar* 10, 11

elephant 25, 32, 35, 56
Ellora caves 56

family shrine 14, 22, 27, 42
fasting 23
festivals 6, 22-23, 42, 60
fish *avatar* 9, 11
flood 9
folk art 6
food 16, 18, 23, 42
forest hermit 8
four classes 12, 16, 19, 29-30, 34, 47, 54, 57-58, 59
four stages of life 8-9, 48
four *Vedas* 47, 60
funeral rites 18-19, 46

Gandhi, Indira 65
Gandhi, Mahatma 4, 14, 21, 23-25, 29, 31, 41, 57, 58
Ganesh 25, 40
Ganga (river and goddess) 26, 52
Ganges river 11, 13, 18, 26, 41, 42, 52
Garuda 27, 59, 62
Gayatri 49
ghee 27, 65-66
Gita, 9, 12-13, 19, 25, 30, 34, 35, 41, 46, 47, 57, 66
the goddess (*devi*) 14, 19, 21, 27, 29, 33, 40, 44, 51, 52, 62
gods and goddesses 4, 5, 14, 19, 21, 22, 25, 26, 27, 28, 29, 33, 34, 35, 39, 40, 43-44, 47, 49, 51, 52-53, 54, 59, 60, 62
grihastha 8
groom 36
gunas 41
Gupta dynasty 5, 6, 30, 50-51
guru 8, 11, 28

Hanuman 28, 44, 54
Harijan 24-25, 29, 58
history of Hinduism 29-31, 68-69
holy man 8, 25, 41, 48, 60, 61
horoscope 32, 36
householder 8, 9
hymns 13, 14, 31, 37, 39, 46, 47, 60, 66

Indra 21, 32
Indus valley civilization 5, 7, 20, 29-30
Islam 6, 31, 38, 44, 47, 55, 57

Jaganatha temple 42
Jainism 4, 30, 58
jati 12, 17
jewellery 21, 36
juggernaut 42

Kali 19, 33, 44, 53
Kalkin 10, 11
kama (one of the three goals of the householder) 8
Kama (god of love) 52
karma 12, 33, 46, 58, 60
Karttikeya 40
Kauravas 12-13, 34, 35, 47
Kshatriyas 12, 17, 34, 47, 59
Krishna 6, 9, 10, 11, 13, 34, 35, 37, 57, 62, 66
Kumbh Mela 42
kurta 20, 21, 36

Lakshmi 9, 11, 23, 35, 62
Laws of Manu 8, 19, 35, 47, 65
linga 53
lungi 21

Mahabharata 12-13, 30, 34, 35, 38, 47, 65
Mahavira 30, 58
man-lion *avatar* 10, 11

mantra 36, 39, 67
Manu 9, 35
marriage 32, 36-37, 46
mathematics 50-51
medicine 50-51
meditation 12, 41, 66
Mira Bai 37
moksha 8, 12, 15, 25, 26, 30, 37, 41, 58, 67
mudra 38
Mughal empire 6
music 13, 38-39, 49
Muslims 6, 31, 38, 55, 57

Nandi 53, 59

Om 39

painting 6
pajama 20
Pandavas 12-13, 34, 35, 47, 65
Parvati 19, 25, 40, 53
paths to salvation 41
philosophy 31, 41, 43, 51, 65
pilgrimage 14, 19, 26, 41-42, 61, 66
pollution, ritual 12, 16, 23, 57-58
pradakshina 42
prashad 55
prayer beads 66
priest 12, 16, 17, 36, 43, 44, 47, 59, 66
puja 7, 14, 21, 22, 23, 42, 55, 60, 65
Puranas 11, 43, 47, 50, 53

Radha 34
Radhakrishnan, Sarvepalli 12, 43
raga 38
Rajjab 57
Rama 9, 10, 11, 22-23, 28, 43-44, 45, 47, 54, 62
Ramakrishna 44-45, 63
Rama with the axe 10, 11
Ramayana 11, 22-23, 28, 30, 38, 43-44, 45, 47

Ramanuja 31, 45
Ram Lila 22-23
Ram Mohun Roy 46
Rani of Jhansi 65
Ravana 11, 22, 23, 28, 44
rebirth 12, 15, 30, 33, 37, 46, 58, 60
Rig Veda 4, 29, 46, 47, 49, 54, 60

sacred books 12-13, 14, 15, 34, 35, 37, 38, 39, 43, 46, 47, 48, 53, 58-59, 60, 65, 66
sacred fire 4, 27, 36, 46, 55, 60, 65-66
sacred places 11, 26, 41-42, 55-56, 66
sacred thread 47, 57
sadhu 48 , 60
salvar-kameez 21
salvation 12, 41
Samkhya 41
samsara 46, 48
sannyasi 8-9, 48
Sanskrit 20, 36, 45, 46, 47, 48-49, 51, 60
Saraswati 14, 39, 49
sari 21, 36
sati 46
science 50-51
sculpture 5-6, 56
shakti 19, 51
Shankara 31, 41, 45, 51
shanti 51
Shesha 62
Shiva 14, 19, 21, 25, 26, 27, 29, 30, 33, 39, 40, 51, 52-53, 56, 59, 60, 61, 62
Shudra 12, 19, 54, 59, 60
shruti 35, 53
Sikh 20
Sita 11, 43-44, 54, 65
Six systems of philosophy 41
smriti 35, 53
soma (drink) 54
Soma (god) 54
songs 13, 14, 37, 39, 60, 66
soul 9, 12, 15, 19, 37, 58
stages of life 8-9, 54, 60

student 8

temple 5, 7, 14, 25, 27, 30, 36, 38, 39, 41, 42, 45, 53, 55-56
tilak 55
time 57
tolerance 57
tortoise *avatar* 9, 10
Tulsi Das 45, 47
turban 20, 37
twice born 47, 57

Untouchables 12, 17, 18, 24-25, 29, 30, 57-58, 59
Upanishads 9, 15, 30, 37, 41, 47, 51, 53, 58-59, 65

vahana 4, 59
Vaishya 12, 17, 47, 59
Valmiki 45, 47
vanaprastha 8
Varanasi 11
varna 12, 16, 17, 18, 30, 34, 54, 57-58, 59, 60
varnashrama dharma 12, 19, 60
Vedanta 41, 51
Vedas 9, 14, 32, 47, 53, 60
vegetarian 4, 18, 23, 25
vehicles of the gods and goddesses 4, 14, 21, 25, 26, 27, 32, 40, 49, 53, 59, 62
villages 6, 14,16, 17, 18, 19, 21, 24, 36, 38, 57-58, 60-61, 63-64
Vishnu 9-11, 14, 19, 21, 26, 27, 30, 34, 35, 42, 43-44, 45, 47, 52, 59, 60, 62
Vivekananda 45, 63

women 8-9, 21, 63-65
World Spirit or World Soul 9, 12, 15, 27, 30, 37, 39, 41, 45, 51
worship 22, 39, 42, 55, 65-66

yantra 66, 67
yoga 12, 29-30, 41, 52, 67
yuga 57